Doctor Wynstock,

Thank you so much for the
many years of great medical
service to my family & me.

Kindest & warmest regards

Tristin K. Llanei.

Excerpts

"Try to imagine this. *No, I mean really try to imagine this.* The normal involuntary reflex to seeing an object, especially a knife, about to hit your body, is to place a hand, arm or something in the knife's path to prevent or repel injury. What if your arms were pinned behind you? You see the knife coming, you feel it puncture and cut your eye the first time and many times thereafter."

" 'On my own time'…I don't care whether or not the defendant can be rehabilitated…His rehabilitation is not an issue…My sympathies are with the victim…Her life is a wreck… Never will she forget the defendant or his sexual attack upon her, whether during the daytime or during nightmares."

"During the presentation, as the defendant sat there smirking, my thoughts were…"

"On certain legal principles, I believe sometimes we intellectualize ourselves into oblivion which often leads to absurd results and injustice."

"Olivia, let me mention…how I must respond to evil is the part of me I wish was unnecessary for you to know, but it is my responsibility, a responsibility I cannot forsake."

Finding Olivia
The Book/The Letters

by

Tristin K. Dawei

authorHOUSE™

1663 LIBERTY DRIVE, SUITE 200
BLOOMINGTON, INDIANA 47403
(800) 839-8640
WWW.AUTHORHOUSE.COM

First published by AuthorHouse 07/13/04

ISBN: 1-4184-2471-4 (e)
ISBN: 1-4184-2472-2 (sc)
ISBN: 1-4184-2473-0 (dj)

Library of Congress Control Number: 2004092954

Printed in the United States of America
Bloomington, Indiana

This book is printed on acid-free paper.

*****

Table of Contents

*****

* * * * *

ACKNOWLEDGMENTS

* * * * *

I would like to recognize my mother who, with very limited resources, gave us love, guidance and encouragement through difficult times.

I would like to recognize my children who have brought a great deal of love and happiness to my life over the years.

I would like to thank Liu Chi-Jen for his gift "Chi Art, The Ultimate Feng Shui Solution." The gift greatly influenced the writing "Finding Olivia The Book/The Letters."

* * * * *

* * * * *

DEDICATION

* * * * *

Wholeheartedly, I dedicate this book and letters to Olivia. I truly am grateful for her being my inspiration to write them. Undoubtedly, she is one of the most magnificent and beautiful people I ever have met.

Tristin K. Dawei

* * * * *

* * * * *

PROLOGUE

* * * * *

Hello. My name is Tristin Dawei. I hope you enjoy reading 'Finding Olivia', but let me offer a caveat at the outset. It is not recommended for persons who are unwilling to allow their actions and thoughts to venture beyond generally accepted scientific principles and tested postulates. Nor is it recommended for those who insist on empirical data to support all hypotheses.

'Finding Olivia' is not for you if you do not believe you were placed on earth for a specific purpose. If you do not believe God, fate, karma, luck and other powers of the universe are able to help you to attain love, happiness and prosperity, you should master your own fate and destiny and not read it.

"Finding Olivia" is for those who are imaginative, creative in thought and actions, and who have a willingness to venture beyond the physical and mental limitations which have been placed upon most of us merely by being born upon the earth.

Most believe the longer we remain on earth and learn from our experiences, the more informed or educated we become. There is truth to this belief. However, I feel it is incomplete for this reason. I believe, as well, that being born here, learning and drawing upon our experiences, necessarily limit our imagination, thoughts and actions to events that occur on earth. As we grow, we become more entrenched in the limitations. Until relatively recently, we almost were completely restricted by earth's boundaries and by the experiences of those who preceded us. We remain severely restricted.

An observation by Grand Master Chi-Jen Liu better will illustrate the point. He will be referred to, from time to time, throughout this book. Chi-Jen Liu supposed if one were to spend his entire existence in a room, the room would become the extent of his knowledge. If the person left the room, he would discover other rooms and that the room was contained within a house. He would discover other houses and a neighborhood. The room then would appear very small. If the person became aware of cities, countries and the earth, the room would appear infinitesimally small. Finally, if he learned the existence of a sun, moon, stars, planets and other galaxies, from his new perspective, he would envision the room as virtually nonexistent.[1]

Allow me to paraphrase the well-known master martial artist, Bruce Lee. He once espoused an idea that one must be completely able to adapt, physically and mentally, to one's circumstances and environment. He used water to be illustrative. Water will conform to the shape of the container in which it is put. Seemingly, it will become amorphous if allowed to escape, when in reality, it has conformed or adapted to the changed influences upon it. The point is that I encourage a completely open-minded reading of 'Finding Olivia' without mental resistance.

[1]

Chi Art. The Ultimate Feng Shui Solution. Chi-Jen Liu, Author. Xlibris, Corp. Copyright, 2002. Page 5.

Independently, I must point out also, that for a full understanding and practical application of some of the principles expressed herein, one must be a romantic, who is open to tenderness and kindness. One with a   keen sensitivity to concepts such as love and fairness. He or she must posses the capacity to share all aspects of his or her life with another without reservation.

* * * * *

AN OVERVIEW

* * * * *

"Finding Olivia" is based, in part, on a true story. It is about a real life judge who, arguably, suffers mental illness. He accedes the suggestion for the sake of moving the story.

The judge is driven and guided by "three meanings." Two of which are the underpinnings for many of his everyday professional decisions. He shares actual courtroom dramas which arose from cases he handled as a prosecutor or judge. The summarized dramas reveal extreme brutality in graphic detail to demonstrate his position on the appropriateness of imposing death in certain cases. Sometimes, he finds himself a little frustrated in meting out punishment in certain other cases because of limitations imposed by law.

The book will show how, from time-to-time, two of "the meanings" conflict with everyday responsibilities and ethical values and how he is able to reconcile the conflicts.

For reasons unknown to him at the time, several months ago, the judge shared "the three meanings"with a young Vietnamese woman whom he met while studying Mandarin Chinese at a local college. After losing contact, he undertook a desperate search for her. He does not know her sir name. He has no address or telephone number for her. He is willing to try all conventional and unconventional means, within the boundaries of the law, 'to find her'. Critical, is his definition of 'find her'. The judge shares paranormal experiences and explores associated activities and possibilities for the purpose of using the experiences and findings for practical application, including 'finding Olivia'. He delves into undeveloped areas of human thought and brain capacity.

He strongly positions that, so long as his mental condition does not cause harm to others, he should be able to be as mentally ill as he cares to be or as his condition may happen to be while 'on his own time.'

If he is insane at times, the story is demonstrative that he is able successfully to shift from insanity to complete lucidity and render reasonable well-founded decisions when required to perform the duties of his office, he thinks.

The "three meanings" as they relate to purpose, love, sex, happiness, depression, and suicide will race the story to an unexpected and dramatic conclusion. "Finding Olivia" will draw upon the imaginations of many and the incredulity of others.

* * * * *

FINDING
OLIVIA

The Book/The Letters
by Tristan K. Dawei

* * * * *

* * * * *

CHAPTER I

A PERSONAL
VIEW

* * * * *

Legends and myths abound, tales, fables and stories are told, poems, ballads and songs have been written and sung throughout the existence of mankind on the subject of love. Philosophers, authors, poets, singers and songwriters have defined love in terms of reaching the highest degrees. Lovers willing to "climb the highest mountain," "swim the deepest sea," "walk the longest distances through the deepest valley, the widest desert." They have written of lovers who endured the strongest wind, rain and snow storms, the most intense heat, cold and other extreme conditions. Some suffered physical and mental pain and hardship. Some were willing to, and indeed, did suffer death for whom he or she loved. The emotion love will comprise a major part of "Finding Olivia" because it is inextricable to 'finding' her. Depression and feelings of incompleteness will be discussed as necessary corollaries. I characterized the following postulates as *"the three meanings." "Evil flourishes when good men do nothing"*[2] *"The mass of men lead lives of quiet desperation"*[3] *and "Love is the active concern for the life and the growth of that which we love."*[4] I did so because I believe they are important for a complete understanding of one's purpose on

[2]

      Burke, Edmond. (1729-1797). 1/9/1795, Letter to Wm. Smith.

[3]

      Thoreau, Henry David. Random House, Inc.   Walden Page 8. Copyright 1937, 1950, 1965, 1992.

[4]

      Fromm, Erich.   Author &Psychologist. The Art of Loving. Harper & Row, Inc. 1956. First Perennial Ed. Copyright 1989, 2000. Harper Collins. Page 25.

earth, what the purpose is, and how to achieve it. That failure to appreciate and achieve the purpose, likely would result in a lifetime of incompleteness. Although some religious teachings, moral standards and political commentary will be foundationally necessary, love and purpose will be the central theme of "Finding Olivia." The book is not intended to preach morals or how one's life should be led. It is not a book on politics. Please be patient on that point.

It is said that love is the most healthy of human emotion and that depression is the least healthy. I suspect most people experience love at least once during their lifetime. Certainly, it is an important factor in man's propagation. I believed I had been fortunate enough to have experienced it. I say so guardedly, because there always seemed to have been a longing for something unknown. Something I could not, at the time, identify. An incompleteness. I imagine many of you readers have experienced similar feelings. Furthermore, in addition to feelings of incompleteness, I experienced great bouts of depression. Studies have demonstrated that most people experience depression of varying degrees throughout life. On that subject, I read and learned a great deal. Health practitioners attribute it to both physiological and environmental factors. But let me make an observation at this point. I was completely, 100 percent cured of depression and incompleteness in every aspect when I met Olivia. I discovered the depression and incompleteness was her absence from my life. I will discuss the significance of her absence later in this writing.

Over the years, I considered biblical principals, teachings and writings of great philosophers and authors on the subject of love, and read some of the greatest love stories ever told. It only is until now however, after having met Olivia, that I realize love's true meaning. It is not my intention here to attempt to surpass the eloquence, feelings, beliefs and expressions of the great writers and singers on the subject. I would not expect to be able to do so. Not because of what I do not feel for her, but because I believe words to be an inadequate medium for my expression of it for her. My point here is that after meeting her approximately eight months ago, it seems, I have been compelled to write my beliefs on the subject. Upon meeting her, I discovered how blindly inadequate I had been at maintaining a good, strong and healthy interpersonal relationship. Perhaps our meeting, stirred and awakened certain attributes which had been part of my character all along. Perhaps our meeting caused me readily to adopt the attributes.

Comparatively speaking to the lovers of old, since meeting Olivia, I am able to say I would be willing to suffer physical and mental hardship for another human being. Her. I would put myself in harms way for her. I would protect the integrity of her body from all harm of whatever type. I would dedicate my life to making her happy. I prefer to be with her at all times. I would be faithful and loyal to her, always have her best interest in mind, and act upon those interests the remaining days of life on earth. I would die for her.

Wow! Those words purportedly convey a strong unequivocal message. I say purportedly because, at first glance, one might say "yeah, yeah, yeah!" Or "yada, yada, yada." All must conclude however, there only are two meaningful choices. They are true. They are not true. If not true, so be it. If true, how could it be so. One purpose for this writing is to demonstrate their truth and why the truth is significant.

Some years ago, I read the Burke passage, "evil flourishes when good men do nothing." I characterized it as one of the "three meanings" because, as earlier mentioned, they are essential to meaningful discussion of 'finding' Olivia. In that regard, I would like to spend the next several pages with the political commentary. As earlier mentioned, it is foundational and, I believe, necessary for a complete understanding of some of this writing's ideas and concepts.

As a paradigm to Burke's postulate, compare George W. Bush and Al Gore. Both impress me as kind and descent men with good intentions. A major difference, however, is for instance, the aftermath of the destruction of the World Trade Center in New York. George W. decided to do something about it. To root out and destroy the evil behind the attack. I strongly believe he should continue to seek and destroy evil whether or not present targets were directly responsible for the Trade Center attack. Recently, there was an article in the N.Y. Times where Gore mentioned Bush was on the wrong course. That it was wrong for the U.S. to blame Hussein for advancing terrorism and to attack the Taliban in Afghanistan. Both are sources of evil. Perhaps, Gore would allow the evil to flourish or, at least, not demonstrate strength in his resolve to abate it. One may argue Bush had a hidden agenda for entering Afghanistan and Iraq. What is certain, however, is the Taliban no longer is controlling, exploiting, raping, torturing and murdering the people of Afghanistan under the guise of religion. What also is certain is Saddam Hussein no longer is exploiting and imposing his will upon the people of Iraq or exporting terrorism.

Consider the   conduct of the, so-called, peace activists in the country, especially during the 60's and 70's. Often, they were misguided students who screamed in protestation of actions taken by the United States Government. In my belief, some were insurgents who had a stake in the war's outcome. They were very effective in manipulation of the students. The actions of the, I would say, very gullible students were tantamount to, for example, a judge who would make a decision without having all the facts. For many, it was popular. Just the thing to do at the time. Nothing more than knee-jerk reactions to circumstances not fully understood. During the Vietnam war, they were able to put enough pressure on Washington that made it politically unfeasible to continue the war, however. Former Presidents Johnson and Nixon backed off and allowed the evil to flourish. There were many good men and women in the country who strongly disagreed with the activists. The difference, however, was the activists were vocal. Many who disagreed remained silent and did nothing. After withdrawal of American forces, *an event celebrated by the activists*, the entire country was taken over. The new regime slaughtered innocent civilians by the tens of thousands not only in South Viet Nam, but Cambodia and Laos as well. Which resulted in the greater evil? The evils of war to prevent evil from spreading or the concession that resulted in mass human destruction? If the former activists were honestly to reflect, I wonder how prudent they now believe their positions were. Certainly, they considered that ten years after the war, the Vietnamese Government announced "Surrender by the north was imminent." "Suddenly, the United States stopped bombing Hanoi." Look at the war on the Korean peninsula during the

1950's and Viet Nam peninsula during the 1960's and 70's. The Korean war wound down without 'help' from activists. Today there is Pyongyang to the north and Seoul to the south. Compare human rights and living standards in each city. As a result of 'help' from the activists during the Viet Nam war, today there is Hanoi to the north and Ho Chi Minh City to the south. No longer is there a Saigon. Compare human rights and living standards in each city. It would seem today's activists would have gleaned something from the lesson.

Everyone appreciates the danger of mentioning politics sometimes, but please try to digest this discussion for a few moments. I say let Bush do his job. He is there for a specific purpose. A recent quote by Bush was *"The Iraqi war was a duty." "Duty sometimes requires the violent restraint of violent men." "In some cases, the measured use of force is all that protects us from a chaotic world ruled by force."*[5] Considering recent events, and after honest evaluation, might one take serious issue with that observation and perspective?

Haven't we all, at one time or another, questioned our purpose on earth? I have, and remain without all the answers. However, after having served twelve years as a lawyer with various prosecution agencies and thirteen as a judge, I have gained important insight on the subject. During the prosecution assignments, I handled many cases that involved murder, rape, robbery, serious violations of children and the helpless, and various other heinous crimes. Oftentimes, the death penalty, life imprisonment and/or decades of imprisonment vigorously were

[5]

NY Times. Front page. Nov. 20th 2003.

sought. Often, and for reasons unknown, I was saddened by the plight of the victim and the victim's family in some of the cases. Their plight seemed to motivate me. I had a sense I could not forego an opportunity to suppress evil.

During the handling of cases where the death penalty was being sought, I spent many nights with heightened brain activity and energy while attempting to sleep. I could not rest until I felt well armored and prepared to, as I called it *"go into a courtroom and do battle with the devil."*[6] I am not *necessarily* implying the lawyer was evil. I am speaking more of the evil deeds. I must mention, however, there were many instances when it was quite apparent the defendant was not alone in his perpetuation of deceit. He was not sophisticated enough to have concocted such an elaborate betrayal.

As a judge, I presided over identically the same charges. Let me mention that I must camouflage my true occupation. I may be a judge, an autopsy surgeon, lawyer, policeman, famous actor, Special Agent of the FBI, psychiatrist who is attempting to cure himself, psychologist who would like to become a psychiatrist, or a mental patient with delusions of grandeur wanting to be any of the above. I do not relish being coy on the subject, however, valid reasons exist why I cannot be candid with you on this point. Please accept my apology.

Also, I would like to mention I structured certain sentences in a fashion that will facilitate accurate translation of the material into Vietnamese, Chinese, Japanese, and Korean languages.

[6]

Dawei, 2003.

As a judge, former prosecutor and human being, I become uncomfortable when justice is not served. Consider the O.J. Simpson case, for example. My personal view is the result was gut wrenching wrong. The case went terribly array for a number of blunders which occurred before and during the trial. I will comment upon one at this time. Unlike Magic Johnson and some of the other super sports figures, Simpson is a Westwood, Bel-Air, Beverley Hills, "westside" type. I am not being pejorative of persons living in those largely affluent areas of westside Los Angeles. I am attempting to put into context his elevated lifestyle. During his heyday, the people of South Central Los Angeles never occurred to him. They were in another world. To him, they were irrelevant. As an example of his deviousness, only during the trial, did the citizens of that community become important. He knew he could capitalize on the sentiment *the case against him was just an attempt to bring down another prosperous Black man.* I do not believe O.J. considered himself to be Black until he needed help from the Black community. Even then, he genuinely did not, but he needed to play the card. He knew many in the community would be awestruck by him and some of the other key players during the trial. He hoped they would be unable or unwilling to fairly evaluate complex scientific evidence. What does a jury of one's peers mean? Persons of the same ethnicity? No. It means a fair cross-section of one's community. Which community was the fair cross-section for O.J.? South Central Los Angeles or Santa Monica where the case should have been tried? Answer. Santa Monica, where people of his affluence would have heard the case. By those who would not have been favorably impressed because of stature. The case should have been tried in the judicial district where the events that gave rise to the charges occurred. There are solid and good reasons why vicinage and venue rules exist. The rules should not be disregarded without a great deal of thought. I believe the decision to move the case by Gilbert Garcetti, the former District Attorney of Los Angeles County, cost him his job. It certainly resulted in a windfall for Simpson.

Another good illustration of the point was the prosecution of Los Angeles police officers for the severe pummeling and beating of Rodney King. The case was shifted out of venue, (out of the county vs. within the county) and tried by a panel more likely to be sympathetic to the defendants. It worked. It seems those jurors were persuaded they could not believe their own eyes after viewing the event on tape.

Let me share one more little tidbit with you and I promise I will move on. Having had the experience of trying murder cases which arose from a violent multiple stabbing, I safely can comment here. During the event, the attacker usually holds onto the victim with one hand and quickly and repeatedly stabs and slashes with the other. The victim, of course, is not standing still. He is moving to avoid injury. Inevitably, the attacker will stab, the back of the hand that held the victim, the attacker's opposing hand. Often, the stabber will cut the inside of the hand that holds the knife. This occurs, as it often does, when the hand slips down onto the blade during the assault. At least according to the civil jury, O.J. repeatedly stabbed and slashed his wife Nicole and Ronald Goldman. Do you think they were standing still while they were being stabbed and slashed? O.J. sold the thought that the cuts on the back of his opposing hand resulted from squeezing a glass after learning of Nicole's death. What a laugh!

Of course, we want to acquit the innocent, however, in my personal view, this was a case where a person who was *guilty in fact* walked free. Simpson was so aware of his guilt, he even was stunned by the jury's verdict. Thereafter, he had the temerity to thumb his nose at society. Do you recall some months after the acquittal, in his warped sense of humor, when he gestured with the knife? Let me ask you, where do you believe O.J. Simpson is right at this moment? In South Central Los Angeles, perhaps involved in charitable causes? Performing a public service? Thinking of how he could perform a public service perhaps? Does he, at the very least feel gratitude toward the community? *I bet you dollars to donuts* the answer to all of the questions is no. They are irrelevant again. I think you know the answer to where he might be. Yes, in Florida with a young, blue-eyed blonde or out on a golf course "trying to find the real killer."

Criminal defense lawyers might respond to my personal view, that justice was served, because the "People" failed to prove the case "beyond a reasonable doubt." Buzz words! Buzz words! Buzz words! Buzz words! Complete unadulterated bull-pucky. What readily comes to mind to most, when learning this, is the often misunderstood and misquoted passage "The first thing we do, let's kill all of the lawyers."[7] The context was the conquerors wanted control without interference by lawyers who may protect their liberties.

7

William Shakespeare, Author. Part II, Henry VI. Page iv. ii.

Undoubtedly, many lawyers play an important and helpful role in society. I believe Johnnie Cochran, for instance, not only is highly skilled at the craft, but is a person of principles and moral character. He did the job the oath required of him. If he could not fulfill the responsibilities required under the oath, ethically, he would not have been able to undertake the defense of the case. As well, lawyers should not decline representation merely because public opinion or sentiment is against it. Lawyers of his caliber serve an important societal function.

My official reply to the assertion the Simpson case was not proven would be, we absolutely are bound by the doctrine "proof beyond a reasonable doubt" as long as the standard is part of our system of jurisprudence. However, no safeguard exists to assure jurors apply the standard. I recall handling a case where jurors, understandably, were furious at a holdout juror who stated, "you already got my brother Tyson, you aren't going to get" the defendant in that case. This juror was completely dishonest in his responses to questions during voir dire. He violated the oath that he would base the decision on the facts and the law. His actions were evil.

Consider the case of Robert Durst, the Texas millionaire who admittedly killed the victim, dismembered his body, thoroughly cleaned the apartment where the killing took place, dumped the body into the Galveston bay, disguised himself, jumped bail and fled the state. Again, like Simpson, Durst was completely stunned upon hearing the not guilty verdict.

My personal view is, because of the many instances throughout the country where jurors arrive at verdicts which clearly are contrary to evidence and common sense, our system needs fixing here. We seriously should consider use of professional jurors. Such utilization would cut down on the glib demagoguery by lawyers, some of whom I refer to as prestidigitators or my coined term, prestidigitationists. Since most readers are familiar with the term, I will not define it here. I included it in the 'Glossary of Terms' for those who may be unfamiliar with it. Seriously, the professional juror concept is not a new idea and is not dissimilar to the grand jury system. Lawyers might say it is against the rules. My reply would be, change the rules if, repeatedly, the result is unjust.

Look at the presumption of innocense that firmly is rooted in our justice system. It sounds so great and noble. Throughout all criminal trials in the country, the accused is presumed innocent. In fact, it is a legal fiction. As a private citizen, my question would be *"If justice and legal purity are the objectives, why presume anything?"*[8]

As earlier mentioned, many lawyers serve an important societal purpose. The government must be made to proceed fairly and prove any case against an accused with competent evidence with sufficient weight to demonstrate the truth of the charge. Some lawyers, however, bring disgrace upon the profession. I recall and instance when a lawyer argued his client's bail should be reduced. That he should be released on his own recognizance. He argued the client had been a holocaust survivor and "I have him caged up like an animal." I disagreed with the appropriateness of an own recognizance release in that his client, while elderly and sympathetic, murdered his elderly wife. I indicated "**I** do not

8

Dawei, 2003.

have your client locked up like and animal," "your client caused himself to be locked up by his misconduct." The lawyer then accused me of antisemitism. The grossly inaccurate accusation was an attempt at intimidation and designed for self promotion. From that day forward, I viewed that lawyer with distrust. Some years later, I heard him present a nearly identical argument to a judge in another case, using the "locked up like an animal" phraseology.

Another example is during the penalty phase of a case, defense counsel began speaking of his personal diagnosis of cancer. The impact it would have on his children if he were not to survive, leaving them without a father. He began outwardly to sob. The sobbing continued for some time. It became very convenient for the defendant to cry at that point. During my response as a prosecutor, I attempted to point out the cancer diagnosis, which had been made ten years earlier, was in remission. That he presented the same argument, with the sobbing, in several other death penalty trials. That his children no longer were minor children. He immediately objected and cried foul.

Another device commonly employed by counsel in cases with heinous facts, was employed in that case during the crying charade. During argument, counsel stood behind the defendant, touched and petted him. Sometimes placing his hands on the defendant's shoulders, neck, arms etc. The purpose was an attempt to deceive the jury by subliminally humanizing the subhuman. This technique is taught at defense strategy seminars.

My personal views are not intended to bring dishonor upon or discredit the court system, judges, lawyers or jurors who honorably performed their civic duties, or others involved in the process. They are not designed to, and I hope they do not, cause anyone who may read this publication to have less confidence in our justice system. All systems evolve and may require periodic adjustment. My view is similar in meaning to the words of the late Justice David Eagleson who served on the Supreme Court of California until 1991. He observed that "Time can be misspent in the pursuit of theoretical elegance...esoteric concepts that the court sometimes put out-ideas that, in an abstract sense, are logical and cohesive-at the level of application, just don't work."[9]

On certain legal principles, I believe *sometimes we intellectualize ourselves into oblivion which often leads to absurd results and injustice. We can achieve justice and legal purity only after decades of systemic societal refinement and scientific and cultural advancement.*[10]

As earlier mentioned, the point of the foregoing was foundational for discussion of purpose on earth. Interesting dynamics of certain cases shed light on what members of the public may be unaware. As well, some of the comments were intended to assist in understanding how persons who appeared overwhelmingly guilty, with a great deal of resources, walked away from two "cold-blooded" murders, when persons of lesser means may not have.

After undertaking responsibility for certain cases some time ago, I discovered and believed my purpose on earth to be to

[9]

Los Angeles Times, Inc. David Eagleson, Assoc. Justice: 1987-1991. May 24, 2003. Pg B30

[10]

Tristin Dawei, August 2003.

respond to evil. Recently, I read a discussion in a book entitled "The Art of Happiness." Written by Howard Cutler, MD, the discussion primarily concerned the wisdom and teachings of the Dalai Lama. After interaction and discussion with the Dalai Lama, the author concluded or seemed to be persuaded that "The purpose for our earthly existence is to seek happiness."[11] He pointed out that during our lives here, we all get a taste of "triumph, despair, joy, hatred and love."[12] That our purpose is to eliminate the negative in order to become or remain happy. I agree that while on earth, we face the obstacles of the negative and the benefits of the positive. I agree most people work hard to eliminate the negative. However, I believe these are the circumstances with which we are faced upon our arrival on earth. The negatives which we strive to overcome, in order to achieve our true purpose.

Because I hold certain personal views, does not mean, I cannot be impartial in my official capacity. We all hold views. Judges are no different in that regard. The difference is judges are duty bound to uphold the law in carrying out the responsibilities of the office in spite of personal views. I have sworn to do that. I would not violate the oath. To do so would, in itself, be evil and, as heretofore stated, I believed my purpose here was to expunge evil.

[11]

The Art of Happiness. Dalai Lama & Howard C. Cutler, MD. Riverhead Books, 1998. Page 16.

[12]

The Art of Happiness. Page 216.

Let me expand a little on the conflicts point. Many judges personally are against abortion or the death penalty. Nevertheless, they may be called upon to make decisions which may be contrary to the personal belief. If the judge cannot separate his personal view from his official duty, he should not hear the case. There is a mechanism, which is utilized from time-to-time, for him or her to disqualify him or herself. Personally, in general terms, I do not believe in therapeutic abortion except for limited circumstances. Rape, incest and health of the mother, for example. This view is in conflict with the controlling law on the subject by the United States Supreme Court, Roe v. Wade.[13] Primarily, the case stood for the proposition that no state may outlaw a medically approved abortion within the first trimester. Many states, however, allow the procedure as late as the ninth month of gestation. Some doctors abort full-term babies who are capable of sustaining life independently from the mother. If the issue presented itself in a case I was required to rule upon, I would be duty bound to rule consistent with Roe v. Wade or decline to hear the case.

Another personal view is a woman should have the right to control her own body. As an added tension, I believe at a certain point in fetal development, for example approximately three months, abortion becomes evil and the woman's right of control becomes subordinate to a child's right to live. I believe in some instances, when a woman exercises the control over her body, she may shape her destiny. Assume for instance, she had an abortion with the consent or encouragement from the would be father. I

13

Controlling legal authority on abortion. Decided by the U.S. Supreme Court, 1973. (7-2).

predict the lives of the, would be parents, would take a tailspin for the worst. They may call it bad luck or chronic misfortune. In fact, a little spirit always would be around them to thwart good fortune. Perhaps this could be alleviated by genuine atonement. Allowing the soul to come to earth by bearing a child may resolve it. This Buddhist teaching was brought to my attention by my second former wife. Certainly, it cannot be disproved.

I do not believe I should be able to impose my personal view on this very private matter. Just as I cannot or should not be able to impose any other of my personal and changing views or beliefs on others. One may argue then, I am in conflict with my duty to oppose evil. Not so, I believe this will be dealt with by a much higher authority than me or any other human being. I must follow the rule of law irrespective of personal views.

This point brings to mind the recent execution of an activist by the State of Florida. The activist was found guilty of murder and the penalty was fixed at death. Admittedly, he killed the victim, a doctor who maintained an abortion clinic. One may argue, was not the activist attempting to prevent evil? My reply would be that in order to maintain an orderly society of any type, rules of law must be recognized. This seems to be true among animals. I believe it was evil, in cold-blood, to kill the doctor. Far less drastic means were available to address the doctor's conduct. On any given day in court, judges hear horrendous sets of facts. Might they become so inflamed by the evil, they pull a firearm and execute the accused right there on the spot?

With some exception, it does not seem to be good practice for the government, (or individuals), to impose its views and determinations of morality and righteousness upon the populace.

An excellent point, I believe, is the Taliban. Fanatical students who had taken over almost a complete country and imposed its sense of morals and religious beliefs, to the extent it did not apply to them. What if George W. were a Shiite Muslim to the point of proactive fanaticism?

On the death penalty subject, persuasive arguments for and against are abundant. As a private citizen, I believe the death penalty an appropriate punishment option in the appropriate case. Let me comment anecdotally. I handled a case where the defendant, who weighed approximately 200 lbs., and was more than six feet in height, along with his associate, who was similar in size and weight, entered a restaurant to rob and extract revenge for the defendant's earlier firing by one of the victims. Three victims were present. A 135 lb. male, the manager, who fired the defendant, and two girls who were in their late teens. The defendant ordered the girls to face and put their hands upon the wall. The defendant's companion then held the male victim from behind pinning his arms as the defendant began to torture him with a butcher's knife. The defendant began repeatedly to jab the victim in the eyes, nose, mouth, cheeks and scalp with the knife. This was intended to inflict pain only at that point. The defendant cut a large chunk from the victim's cheek. He embedded the knife deeply into the victim's shoulder. He drove it from the outside of the victim's leg completely through to the inside where it hit the victim's genital area. At that point none of the thirty or so wounds were particularly life-threatening, just extremely painful. One of the female victims survived the attack. After being stabbed by the defendant, she fell to the floor and feigned death while continuing to receive more stab wounds being inflicted by the defendant. She said during the stabbing of the torture victim, screaming continued on-and-on for many minutes. I suppose like a lifetime for the victim. Try to imagine this. *No, I mean really try to imagine this*. The normal involuntary reflex to seeing an object, especially a knife, about to hit your body, is to place a hand, arm or something in the knife's path to prevent or repel injury. What if your arms were pinned behind you. You see the knife coming, you feel it puncture and cut your eye the first time and many times thereafter. You see it and feel it as it penetrates your face, cheek and scalp. You feel what remains of the destroyed eye fall upon your cheek. With your remaining eye, you see your blood rushing out and begin to blur your remaining vision. You are completely helpless to stop the attack. You have absolutely no control over the brutal destruction of your body. The pain experienced being so intense, you are about to go into shock. The victim was not in shock at that point, however. As evidenced by the screaming, he continued to feel the extreme pain. Finally, there was complete silence. This testimony was consistent with the autopsy surgeon's forensic finding, the knife then was plunged into the victim's neck and throat and exited the other side. The thrust completely severed the larynx, the "voice-box." At that point the victim no longer had the ability to scream. Nevertheless, he did not die until several minutes later as he lay on the floor and asphyxiated from his blood that filled his lungs. Next, the defendant proceeded to stab the first female victim. While she faced the wall, the defendant plunged the knife into her back with such force, the tip of it exited just below the skin of her breast. The defendant then spun her around and plunged the knife into her abdomen.

According to the autopsy surgeon, the knife did not twist because of the victim's falling to the ground, but because the defendant voluntarily twisted it. This victim deceased. The defendant then proceeded to stab the third victim who, as earlier mentioned, survived the attack. The co-defendant who held the victim during the stabbing, received life imprisonment without the possibility of parole. During an interview, he stated the defendant, stabber "went off on those people with the knife." Consider if one of the kids had been your son, daughter, niece, nephew, brother, sister, other family member or friend and early that morning law enforcement officials knocked at your door and delivered that news. You then were given the detail on how the child died. By the way, the stabber had cuts to both of his hands. Frankly, I would like to have tried the case in China where justice is swift and certain. This comment is not an affront to the justice systems of either country. It is to touch upon the observation that *in our quest to achieve legal purity, we sometimes are led to absurd results.*

It is because of conduct of that severity that I believe the death penalty to be appropriate. In my private capacity as a citizen/voter, I strongly advocate it as I do abolition of abortion after about three months. If the death penalty does not deter others, certainly it would deter him. I equate it to cancer. If you put it in remission, analogous to say life imprisonment, it would resurface and kill again, in or outside of the prison. The cancer must be killed. Further, I believe neither the death penalty nor life imprisonment without the possibility of parole adequately address certain atrocious misconduct. Death would give instant relief, perhaps. Life imprisonment without the possibility of parole would allow him to continue to breathe, eat and exist. To be maintained by society at taxpayer expense. My proscription for misconduct of that magnitude would involve a period of physical hardship, including corporeal punishment, before execution.

I view individuals such as the defendant in that case as nonhuman, as subhuman. I believe there are those among us who are demons or ghosts disguised as human beings. Take for example, a sampling. Hitler, Pol Pot, and the torturers of DEA agent Enrique Camarena.

Perhaps some readers have reservation on the appropriateness of the death penalty for any case. Again, I feel compelled to back-up my assertion that life imprisonment without the possibility of parole just does not work for many cases. I will proceed with another true case.

During mid-October, after being released from prison in May of the same year for manslaughter, the defendant entered a public park where three teenaged boys and girls were drinking beer and smoking marijuana. The defendant proclaimed the park to be his and ordered the youngsters to leave. After verbal challenges by the boys, the defendant grabbed one of them in a head-lock fashion. He pulled a gun from his waistband and discharged it into the boy's cheek. He discharged it a second time into the boy's eye, killing him. He dropped the boy to the ground. The defendant then grabbed a second boy in a similar fashion and discharged the firearm into his eye, killing the second boy. The defendant then fired numerous shots at the third boy who attempted to flee the park. The third boy was struck three times. He attempted to shoot the girls who took refuge in a car.

Approximately two weeks later, on October 31, the defendant entered the home of a couple with whom he had a previous acquaintance. He believed they provided information to law enforcement concerning the park murders. Because of the acquaintance, the defendant was able to take them unaware. The first victim was the husband. The evidence revealed he was seated in a recliner with the defendant stooped next to him. The defendant produced a handgun and discharged it twice into the face of the victim. The defendant then stood over him, touched the barrel of the gun to the top of his head and delivered the "coup de grace." A total of three gunshots to the head at close range. At the time of the shooting of the first victim, his wife apparently had been on the couch reading a novel. At the crime scene, one of her slippers was located on the floor pointed in the direction of the door. A few steps ahead was a second slipper and a novel. A few feet ahead, in close proximity to the door was her body lying in a pool of blood. She sustained three gunshot wounds to the side of the head and neck. The case was handled during my tenure as a prosecutor. The defendant, who was a hardcore gang member with multiple prior convictions, appeared in front of the jury looking like a college student. He wore glasses, a shirt and tie with a sweater over. He had a difficult time covering the numerous tattoos which covered a great deal of his upper body. The difficulty was covering those which extended above his collar and onto his upper neck. He carried a Bible daily. During my years in the courtroom as a lawyer and judge, I found it very common for the accused to appear before the jury wearing a crucifix. It's as if the jail sells them. Fortunately, in this case, the farce did not work, but consider the numerous cases in which it did. In addition to his evil on the outside, this vile subhuman attempted to have one of the witnesses killed during the trial to prevent his testimony. The jury returned a verdict of death. After numerous appeals, the decision was sustained by all appellate courts, including the U.S. Supreme Court. However, pursuant to federal rules of criminal procedure, a federal judge intervened and overturned the death verdict while leaving the conviction in place. Brief mention of the Bible by the prosecution in response to the defense argument to the jury "how could you vote to kill the defendant, you are not God" was the reason for upsetting the death verdict.

The new prosecutor on the case could not persuade a key witness to testify during a retrial. The defendant's penalty then became life without the possibility of parole. A few years after conviction, the defendant achieved a ranking position in a prison gang hierarchy. He ordered a 'hit', (a killing), on a fellow inmate. The prosecution was unable to persuade prison inmate witnesses to testify. What would you expect if such a witness did testify? In front of the next jury, the defense would have a great time talking about the crime that put the inmate witness in prison, thereby, shifting blame away from the defendant for the murder. To cause the jury to spend its time and energy on the witness's crime and not the facts that would convict his client. A common ploy. The theme of the prosecution's response in such cases usually only can be "if a crime were committed in hell, you would not expect to have angels as witnesses." Apparently, the defendant has been given a free pass on that killing.

Another regularly used ploy is to shift the blame to the police agency for shoddy investigation. Sound familiar? I ask you to tell me what the punishment should be in the aforementioned case. As in the case that involved the torture, I would relish the opportunity and discretion to fashion his punishment. It would involve physical pain and hardship, before his execution. Would it be "cruel and unusual punishment?" What about the suffering by the victims and their families?

Judges do not have sufficient power to do, in my view, what ought to be done to him and others who commit such heinous crimes. At this point, he continues to eat, breathe, exist and kill. Likely, he will kill again. The cancer should be eradicated.

This is a good vs. evil proposition. Evil's encroachment, has become more than mere encroachment. Consider this. Why not go along with removing "One Nation Under God" from the pledge of allegiance? Why pledge allegiance? While we are at it, let's remove "In God We Trust" from our currency and any other suggestion the country was founded upon Judeo-Christian principles. I believe the principles upon which it was founded, caused America to achieve its greatness. I believe these latest proposals are an attempt to strip the country of all morals, values and decency. To cause it to become an atheist society. Consider the ACLU (American Civil Liberties Union) types, for example. Their syrupy whining is causing the country to go to hell and become God forsaken. They rejoice when a killer of multiple victims is spared the death penalty or released from prison. Ostensibly, the group's purpose is the protection of individual liberties. In fact, they have caused the taking away of individual liberties. Release of a maniacal killer reduces the liberties of the law-abiding citizen. His security. Championing the causes of racial hate groups, ostensibly for preservation of individual liberties (of evil doers), infringes upon the liberty of others. The targets of their hatred. The law abiding is less secure to move about. I believe the group's true purpose is to achieve atheism and erode the inner and outer strength of the country. To weaken its fiber. To cause it to be more vulnerable to those who are bereft of values. The group is effective because our government is structured where it's activities must be tolerated. The group's aim, however, is to weaken the government. Do you really believe if a Nativity, Menorah, Buddha, Koran or any other religious icon were placed on public property, no longer would there be separation of church and state? Or that it even remotely is a threat of such? Nonsense! These are liberties the subversive group is attempting to destroy. We have had "In God we Trust" on our currency since I can remember. It is part of our heritage. Church and state continue to be separate, don't they?

Sometimes it seems even the smallest thing that happens in life has meaning or purpose. A long time childhood friend tipped me to a great Alan Jackson selection I was listening to the other day. It is entitled "Where Were You When the World Stopped Turning." [14]The song is about September 11th.[15] It reminded me of decency and wholesomeness that America is about. That leaders like George W. are trying to preserve and the fanatics and ACLU types are attempting to erode.

[14]

Greatest Hits, Volume II. #15. Alan Jackson, perf. Arista, 2003.

[15]

September 11, 2001, date World Trade Center Complex, NY, USA was destroyed.

I promised this writing would not be about politics. Perhaps you now are wondering. I continue to maintain that it is not. Unfortunately, a political undertone is necessary. I don't like it either. Please bear with me for a few more pages on this stuff.

Consider this one. The other day I read an article where the doctor who was accused of using his medical skills to keep DEA Agent Enrique Camarena alive to suffer more torturing, filed a lawsuit against the United States Government on the basis it's agents should not have returned him to the United Sates for prosecution. Do you believe he deserves millions of U.S. dollars for that? What would happen if the event had been committed by an American upon a Mexican agent and the American was taken to Mexico? Do you believe the Mexican high court would have let the American go? After his release, would he then be permitted to return to Mexico and file a lawsuit for millions of pesos? Other countries are not playing by the same rules. Is our legal system to become the biggest joke of the world? Let our law enforcement do what ought to be done under those circumstances. There should be reciprocity of rules of law. A foreign national should be prosecuted and subject to punishment and procedure using the laws of his country. Oh no, we cannot search those coming into the country who look like terrorists, walk like terrorists, act like terrorists. We must pretend we do not recognize them or their purposes. Give them a student visa, social security number and drivers license and wait until they blow up something. God forbid the government take prophylactic measures, even if their status no longer is valid. That would be unfair. After something is blown up, give them a lawyer at taxpayer expense so the insanity defense can be asserted. *"Men never do evil so completely and cheerfully as when they do it from religious conviction."*[16]

The good men and women of this country should let their voices be heard. Stop the nonsense of a vocal few activists who dictate how society will live. George W. and subsequent presidents who share his values, should continue doing what ought to be done. Strong leadership in this area is essential to the country's physical integrity and sovereignty. One observation. They are not stupid fanatics. Doubt if they would do the same in China where strong resolve and common sense prevail in this area.

Of course separation of church and state is prudent. One need not look very far back in history, and in some country's today, to be reminded of the abuses perpetrated by the state under the guise of religion. This does not mean all our moral principles should be abandoned, however. We have been given "a heads up" by the destruction of the World Trade Center, in my belief. Keep eroding and removing God's presence from the country and evil will flourish under the pretext of something else being called God.

For the pure at heart ACLU types, it is another instance of *intellectualizing into oblivion and leading to absurd results. For the evil at heart ACLU types, it is another instance of intentionally attempting to cause evil to flourish.*[17]

* * * * *

[16]

Pascal, Blaise: Pensees.(1632-1662). French mathematician, physicist and religious philosopher.

[17]

Dawei, Fall 2003.

* * * * *

CHAPTER II

THE INTRODUCTION

* * * * *

I began writing "Finding Olivia" during August. I first met her during a Mandarin language Chinese course at a local college at the beginning of a Spring semester. I noticed her the first day, but assumed her to be a child because most in the class were late teens or very young adults. One day she came to me and said she was not one of the youngsters. She did appear slightly older, but barely. She said she was an accountant. That she was attending night school to improve her Chinese speaking and writing skills. She explained she was not ethnic Chinese, however, but Vietnamese. She said her name was Olivia. That being the first time in close proximity to her, coupled with her exotic name, I was stunned by her beauty. I was pleasantly surprised she stopped to share her thoughts with me.

For important reasons, human societies consist of many attractive women and men to varying degrees. Pairing purposes is one good reason. There was something strangely eye-catching about Olivia, however. At that time, I did not know why. I found myself being unable to stop watching her or noticing her presence or absence. I will explain this later. I recall a time when the professor asked for volunteers for an oral presentation. Of course, I always went first. The youngsters being too intimidated. After my presentation, there were no more volunteers. After a long pause, I asked the professor might I volunteer the next speaker. I did so to break the ice. As I scanned the classroom, I already knew I wanted to call on Olivia. I then thought, it would be too obvious. I therefore, deliberately selected someone other than Olivia. Later, I regretted I did not go along with my feelings.

Routinely, I would arrive early to take advantage of the quiet empty classroom to continue preparation for the evening's class. Her pattern was to arrive fifteen to twenty minutes after the class had gotten underway. Again, to my pleasant surprise, she began to arrive thirty minutes or so before class began. I could have been wrong, but I suspected it was a purposeful change. Eventually, we began to talk about things such as her work, her objectives, my work, etc. One day, however, she stopped attending. For some reason, I became apprehensive. Thinking, what if she dropped the class? What if I never see her again? I could not determine why it was so important to see her again. I hardly knew her, I thought. I asked of her through a fellow classmate, the only other student who was older than just beyond high school age. The classmate provided me with her cell phone number. It was as if I hardly could wait until class was over, whereupon, I dialed with great anticipation. With great anxiety and despair, however, I discovered the number no longer was in service. I sat through the next two sessions without her being present. She always was on my mind, for reasons unknown to me at the time. I decided, I would withdraw from the class, but would give it one last chance. One evening, I waited near an entrance to the building. As five, ten and finally fifteen minutes or so lapsed, I had given up hope of ever seeing her again. As I turned to leave, the main door opened. It was Olivia. Although casually attired, she was strikingly beautiful. I asked where she had been. I told her I attempted to reach her by phone and her classmate associate had not seen or heard from her. She explained she had become very ill. I heard the lingering congestion as she spoke. As she turned to rush to class, I stopped her and explained I would not be attending that night, and asked if I could see her.

Her reply was no. I wondered why. Instantaneously, I inquired "do you have a boyfriend?"

She said "yes."

For some unknown reason, I did not believe her.

Following the next class in which I attended, again I asked if I might speak with her. Reluctantly, she gave me a rough time limit of 30 minutes. I could sense there may be some flexibility there, however. One of my first inquiries was, "do you love him?" It was clear I was referring to her earlier response that she had a boyfriend.

Her response was "of course I do." "I would not be with him if I did not love him."

I began to revisit some of the things I mentioned in earlier conversation, such as purpose and motivation. Also, I reintroduced "the three meanings." She seemed perplexed when I shared with her the "first meaning," Burke's "evil flourishes" maxim.

A good example of its illustration was in a 1970's Universal Picture entitled "High Plains Drifter"[18] which starred actor Clint Eastwood who played the town Marshal. For the most part, the populace comprised cowards. Precipitating the movie's thesis was a group of ruthless outlaws who rode into town and bullwhipped the marshal to death. Most of the towns people watched the beating from places of hiding. None dared to intervene. The marshal was interred at the outskirts of the town limit without a grave marker.

[18]

Universal Pictures, Hqd. 100 Universal City Plaza
Universal City Calif.

One day, the marshal's ghost rode into town disguised as a "drifter." He warned that the outlaws, who had beaten him to death, soon would be released from prison and returning to take over the town. The cowardly populace, of course not having the courage to defend themselves or even their loved ones, nor abate any other type of evil, made an arrangement with the drifter to take on the gang. He agreed to do so, but conditioned his help on gaining their assistance. He tried building their courage by showing them how to use firearms. He conducted a dry run. The practice run was a complete failure and further highlighted their cowardice. The drifter decided to teach a lesson. He harassed and intimidated them to the farthest extreme. He took over the town hotel and the hotel owner's wife. The owner was too cowardly to object. Eventually, the people mustered enough courage to formulate a plan to rid themselves of the drifter. A plan which itself was cowardly. One night, they entered the drifter's room and began repeatedly to strike him with clubs as he slept. Needless to say, only a bedroll was in the bed. As the drifter watched their cowardly attempt, he ignited a stick of dynamite and tossed it into the room. All escaped, but the hotel was completely destroyed. The owner sobbed at the loss.

Finally, the outlaws arrived and began to employ their plan. The drifter however, of course without the assistance of the towns persons, gunned them down. He then demanded that the town be painted red, to signify "hell." They complied. He rode away as the newly appointed marshal, a dwarf who had shown some courage with his limited abilities, properly marked the grave site of Marshal Duncan. The drifter then faded into the desert.

I believe another good example of the importance of the "first meaning" was contained in a L.A Times newspaper account the other day. A victim was being repeatedly stabbed by gang members near a fast food restaurant. Although the restaurant no longer was open for business, some of its employees still were present. After the attack, the victim ran to the restaurant for assistance. As he pounded on the door and windows in deperation, an employee acknowledged his presence and bloody physical condition. The employee refused to allow the victim to enter and refused to notify law enforcement or medical personnel. The reason given for the refusal was he was an illegal entrant and did not want any attention drawn to him. That he would risk deportation by summoning police and medical officials to the location. My reaction was a person of his moral character should be deported. Why should persons of his caliber be allowed to remain in the country? If he were to return after deportation, jail him and deport him again.

I drew upon the Thoreau principle to explain the "second meaning" to Olivia. "The mass of men lead lives of quiet desperation."[19] Years earlier, I discovered I fit squarely within the ambit of that observation. How often have you done the same? Something being very important to your life. Something which could have been life altering in a positive way. The potential to bring love, happiness, prosperity. Nevertheless, you remained silent. As you pondered whether you should do or say something, you knew it was an excellent opportunity, but you allowed it to pass. "It will come around again," you thought. "Maybe next

[19]

Walden & Other Writings.

time," you thought. You remained silent and grieved. The grief turned into desperation. Perhaps, you still haven't learned. Perhaps, this is the way you continue to live your life, "in quiet desperation." If so, that is too sad. I know. I did it for years.

I decided not to accede to it on this important occasion and I let her know why. I ventured into all "three meanings" at that time because I wanted her to feel safe with me. I did not want her to feel threatened in any way, and I wanted her to know my motive and intentions were good. She was wide-eyed when I explained, when I first met her, it seemed to be "love at first sight." That I had to avoid looking at her to stay composed. At this point, she asserted she was aware of this tension. I told her when she gave her presentation, she touched my heart. She injected "that is easy to say."

Actually, it was easy to say because it was true. Usually, only untruths are difficult to state. I told her I had the option of remaining silent, to do nothing, allow the term to conclude, never to see her again, without her ever knowing how I felt. In other words, to "live in quiet desperation." I explained my second option, which I exercised, was to let her know, to the extent possible, in the time frame she allowed, how I felt about her. The worst that could happen was to learn she did not feel the same. Within approximately thirty minutes, I attempted to explain the ideas "evil flourishes when good men do nothing," "the mass of men lead lives of quiet desperation" and "the concept of love" which segues into the third and final explanation to her that evening.

The author, Eric Fromm, described love as a concept in his book entitled "The Art of Loving." He observed love to be *"the active concern for the life and the growth for that which we love."* [20] For some reason, the definition stayed with me for several years. It seems, however, I never really employed it, nor did I ponder or explore its true meaning. During the many years of my immaturity, I must admit in some aspects I still refuse to grow up, I thought if she were cute, the spark, excitement and intimacy were there, and you enjoyed spending most of your time together, it must be love. Albeit, much later in life and after years of failed relationships, I truly considered the "active concern" postulate. It was an enlightening and humbling experience. One day, the description hit me in the heart like a harpoon. As a Frenchman might say, "coup de foudre." If any of you have watched John Madden on Monday Night Football, undoubtedly, you would have heard him describe the execution of a play and then the result as "...then boom." It is that type of hit I am trying to describe here.

Fromm's description also brought to mind certain lyrics from Elton John who is one of my favorite recording artists. For many years, John collaborated with talented Bernie Taupin in song writing. I do not know whether Taupin and/or John authored the lyrics, but he must have, as they say, "been there, done that." The lyrics were "the instant that you love someone, the second that the hammer hits." "....the pieces finally fit."[21] When one experiences the sensation, it becomes un-mistakenly clear. You know it is not a casual relationship. One will appreciate

[20]

The Art of Loving. Fromm.

[21]

Love Songs. Elton John, performer. 1996, "The One."
MCA Records. Universal City, CA.

the obligations owed the person loved and gladly and willingly undertake the responsibility. Continuing, I drew upon Fromm's invaluable enlightenment that night and related to her what love meant to me and how it translated into my present feelings and what my responsibility would be to her. Actually at that time, I no longer believed in the concept, "love at first sight." I was not, however, being untruthful with her nor would I ever be. I will explain later. I explained love meant maintaining an active role in assuring her physical and mental well-being. From the top her head, her hair, her eyes, her high cheek bones, her skin, the shape of her chin line, her nose and mouth, her body-shape, her arms, slender hands and fingers, her legs and her feet. Meaning, I would be responsible for maintaining the integrity of all that comprised her. I said I would put myself in harms way for her. I said perhaps one day there may be a sickness which may cause her to be confined to bed. During that time, she may need assistance to the toilet. I would carry her there, wait there for her, clean her up, bathe her, carry her back to bed and remain with her and do all possible to aid her recovery. That I could not be happy until she recovered. I continued that it means, I may be at work conducting very serious court business and from time-to-time, throughout the day, thoughts of her would occur to me and bring a smile to my face. That I hardly could wait the end of the work day to rush home to see her. As I walked through the door, she would be there waiting my arrival and very happy to see me. I hardly could wait to hug her. To enjoy the aroma of what was being prepared by her for dinner. To sit there and enjoy having the dinner with her and thereafter, going hand-in-hand, for a walk. Perhaps, going out for dinner, truly enjoying her company. It meant to enjoy the leisure of Saturday morning after waking and having breakfast by the pool with her. Perhaps preparing a breakfast in bed for her. On Saturday evening we might cuddle and watch a movie. Perhaps go out for a glass of wine and a little dancing. As I take her hand and lead her to the dance floor on the most beautiful and romantic ballad, I would hold her and feel I was at the exact place, at that very moment in time with the very person I desired to be with more than any other person in the entire world. Upon our return home and getting into bed, experiencing her love never could be compromised and my love so solid and absolute there never would be an appetite to do so. I recognized life may throw circumstances which may cause either of us to suffer a grievous loss or condition which may cause mental anxiety or pain. I assured her I would be there to comfort her and do all in my power to alleviate and ease the pain. She was awestruck and speechless at this time. She only said "whoa, you have laid a lot on me."

She then became self deprecating. She said "people say I do not smile enough," "my English is not very good, especially in your circles."

I replied "you are so beautiful to me as you are." "During judicial functions, never could there be anyone present I possibly could care for as much as I care for you." "I would be so proud of you."

With perhaps the cutest expression I ever had witnessed, she jokingly said with a partial smile "but you're the judge."

Perhaps, I should have, however, I did not allow her to further respond. I felt a little pressed for time. I said, you know, I realize it is not necessarily so that you could feel the same for me. If you do not or cannot, you should not feel guilt. "If you don't, you just don't." "It is either there or it isn't." "Nothing could change that." "It would not be your fault." "Fault would not be an issue." "I only want to help you uncover your feelings." I mentioned that at that point because I was reminded of Grand Master Liu's words *"when no spark exists between a man and woman, it is useless if the man is hot and the woman is cold, it is hopeless when the woman is hot and the man is cold."*[22] In addition, I wanted to give her an out. At one point, I inquired "would it be impossible for you to love a man like me?"

She looked at me and pondered for a few seconds and responded: "well it would not be impossible, but..."

This comment was encouraging coupled with the fact that on at least two occasions during the conversation, she interjected she really did not have a boyfriend. Finally, she told me her age. I was somewhat pleased, but hoped she would be just a few years older.

When I contemplate life with Olivia, I think never would I lose sight of her importance to me. I always would address her with kindness and softness. I always would be conscious of and sensitive to her needs whether or not they are apparent. During stressful times, I would see her as my relief, my comfort, my reason for living and the love of my life and hereafter.

22

Chi Art, The Ultimate Feng Shui Solution. Page 35.

*****

CHAPTER III

THE UGLY
HEAD

*****

As earlier mentioned, I asked Olivia whether it would be impossible to love a man like me. I wanted her to deeply ponder the question. I believe she did so. As she pondered, and before she could respond with any conclusion. Intentionally, I threw out other considerations. Some of the things I asked were, "does it matter I am not Vietnamese?" "Olivia, I would need your heart." "You must consider whether there is anything about my physical appearance which does not please you." "When you look upon my face or into my eyes, my hair, when you see my shape and build, you must truly enjoy and love what you see and feel." Sensing the type of person she is, the type not wanting to hurt the feelings of another, I continued by saying, "If you do not feel those things, however, it would not be your fault. It is nature's ordering." It reminded me of a scenario posited by Garth Brooks who is another favorite recording artist and country singer. In one of his songs, the lyrics were to the effect *she loves and longs for him, he loves and longs for another who in turn loves and longs for someone else.* I tried to explain to Olivia this is a healthy pairing necessity. I characterized it as such because it must be present to maintain an orderly society.

Olivia responded to the first question which concerned ethnicity in almost a hurt fashion. She said "Tristin, you know I am not like that."
Watching her expressions and hearing the tone of her voice, all of which exuded honesty and purity, in itself, touched my heart. I felt sorry for propounding the question.

During this encounter with Olivia, I was reminded of when a child is born. It possesses no biases, meanness or prejudices. Sometimes I analogize the newborn to a blank computer which is programed to respond to data it perceives through at least five, and if the child is fortunate, six senses.

Olivia's pureness of heart along with her overall beauty and makeup almost instantly drew me to her. One might ask "is not concern for beauty or good looks shallow and superficial?" Let's put it this way. During any life cycle, why do two particular species of birds, fish, or other animals that recognize monogamy, select one another and not another? It, indeed, is *in the eye of the beholder and the beholder's eye is set as it is by nature*[23]. Appearance is the plume or bright feather that attracts another of its species. Once the attraction occurs for introductory purposes, the relationship may begin to build based upon all the overall qualities determined to exist between them.

Because of the foregoing discussion, perhaps you are thinking, this chapter should have been entitled "The Beautiful Woman." Well, it is entitled "The Ugly Head" because I would like to touch upon the dynamics of ethnicity in courtroom and other settings. The expression is *"racial hatred and intolerance again has raised its ugly head."* As we proceed, I ask you to keep in mind, it is not possible to address this vast subject matter in more than a thumbnail sketch.

Earlier, I mentioned judges may hold certain personal views which potentially conflict with carrying out the duties of the office. Of course this is true with most human beings. Unfortunately, the ethnicity of persons appearing before the courts is not off limits to decision making or the manner in which testimony is given, whether intentionally or subliminally. It is

[23]

Dawei, 2003.

my overall sense, however, most judicial and police officers are honest in that regard to the extent possible. I couch it in 'to the extent possible' terms because even those with honorable intentions sometimes inadvertently may feed into old prejudices and stereotypes.

Let me give an example. In court, on a daily basis, one may hear a police officer testify in the following fashion pursuant to a question by a deputy prosecutor pertaining to the identity of the perpetrator. "Yes, it is the male Black seated at counsel table wearing the blue jail clothes." Or when describing pertinent events, "I saw three male Blacks standing in the courtyard." However, when the accused are Caucasian, the testimony usually is "yes, it is the man seated at counsel table wearing the blue jail clothes"or "I saw three men standing in the courtyard." Clearly, a racial description is needed in certain circumstances, however, it would seem irrelevant, though prevalent, in this context. It is unknown what impact, if any, such description may have on a trier-of-fact, judge or jury. Hopefully, none.

I recall being present at an informal setting when, during 'his own time', a judge gave the following account of a Black person. "He was a great big burly..." When the judge realized persons of other color were present he added, "a good-looking thing." It is difficult for a good man to respond and educate one on this type of thinking, but we sure strive to do so. I have heard it said this judge "is not one of the sharper knives in the drawer." I added that comment to give a sense his views are not too prevalent within judicial circles.

On a grander scale, let's be honest, not mince words, and call it the way that it was. Certainly, I am aware of the popularity of former President Reagan, but 'don't shoot the messenger'. Ronald Reagan did great things for the country on a global scale. However, I believe he harbored racial animus. This harboring seemed to fortify the racial tension in the country at that time. Contrast former President George H. W. Bush. It was necessary for George H. W. to come up with "Kinder Gentler America" and "Compassionate Conservative" notions out of the political realities and racial climate that, at the time, existed. I believe racial inequality runs against the grain and character of George H. W. I believe the same can be said of son, President George W. Nearing the end of Reagan's second term, I sensed a tension between Reagan and Bush on that issue. It is shameful it is an issue which a President must contend in the United States as late as 2004.

It is perplexing that a mortal human being, somehow is of the belief the color of his exterior makes him superior. That there is an entitlement. The belief apparently has no correlation to content of good character, nor consequences. In not much longer than 75 years, it will decease and return to the dust. The superiority tenure will be no more. The soul that was housed by the exterior will not decease, however. The evil deeds will be judged. Perhaps the individual will be required to return to earth as a target of racial discrimination, if he or she is lucky. Judges must and will be extremely accountable. If he intentionally made even one decision based upon racial hatred or ignorance, one could imagine the severe consequences when the judge is judged.

Before I go on and on with the 'ugly head' subject matter, I would like to cut it short by asking a few questions and raise a hypothetical question or two. What is the ethnicity of most persons in our prison facilities? What ethnic groups in the country have the highest percentage of unemployment? Which groups have the highest percentage of persons living at or below poverty level? What was the financial profile of all prison inmates before incarceration? What were his or her employment prospects? What educational opportunities were available to him or her? Hypothetical question: what if all the wealth in the United States were redistributed. For instance, to cause all unemployed, homeless and poor people to acquire wealth or at least middle-class sufficiency? Is it likely then crime and imprisonment rates would remain the same? Is it likely that persons who are able adequately to support their families would enter the corner liquor store to rob the proprietor? What if, not only, wealth is bestowed upon the underprivileged, but it is shifted away from the privileged? Would their *sense of justice* values change? If America were to address its weaknesses, *not just lip-service, but really address them*, it would become an even greater country. What are the weaknesses? (1) Disparity in wealth, (2) racial animus, and (3) crime. Greed causes the disparity. Ignorance and evil cause the hatred. Crime is a result of the two. Clearly, the solution is not rocket science. *The first thing we shall do is cut off the 'ugly head' and let its green blood flow.*

I will discuss how justice interfaces with leniency, compassion and mercy later in this writing.

45

*****

CHAPTER IV

THE OLD CLICHE
'LOVE AT FIRST SIGHT'?

*****

I tried to study her face for as long as possible during our second encounter. I wanted it to become indelibly etched into my memory, an inextricable part of me. She is like an undiscovered beautiful and precious jewel. Let me describe her face in poetic terms. The soft facial bone structure is complemented with high smooth cheekbones and well-sculpted jaw and chin lines. The nose and mouth are masterfully and artfully molded. Her brown eyes sparkle and have been mounted on a rich creamy layer of skin. I recall her bright glowing aura and countenance. It seemed she radiated energy while exuding innocence and naivete. I would say, if angels in fact appear as we envision them, Olivia has the face of one. I do not believe her beauty could be replicated by an artist's brush. If ever revealed, I believe Hollywood also would be trying to find her.

Readers in the Chinese community, undoubtedly, are familiar with Teng Li Jen or Teresa Teng. My opinion is she is one of the most magnificent performers of modern time. She is moving of the spirit and soul cross-culturally. One would get a good idea of the overall countenances of Olivia, by viewing tract twenty-two of a music video performed by Teresa wherein she sang "The Power of Love."[24] It seems Olivia could have been Teresa's reincarnate. The countenances are striking. During each time I viewed the performance, I felt a slight chill.

I specifically recall intently looking at Olivia and thinking, what if I never again see her. On the other hand, it seemed I knew that I would. It would be tens of thousands of times better

[24]

Teresa Teng Digital Versatile Disc. Polygram Records, Ltd., 1995.

than Christmas if Olivia could reciprocate the feelings I have for her. The only way I could imagine her touch, to say the least, is "breathless." I walked Olivia to her car that night. I was a bit piqued when I saw the last three digits of her license plate, 515. Earlier, she indicated her birth day and month to be 3/6. The numbers and combinations thereof have seemed to surprise, bewilder and/or plague me throughout the years. A daughter from a previous marriage was born 6/15 and another, 5/15. I recall an instance when after an ATM transaction, my account balance was 1555.36. I recall a time being almost desperate for a deal on a house. The realtor had one final property to show which had fallen into foreclosure. Instinctively, I knew it was the perfect house. I made an offer which was accepted. The address was 1556. Once my satellite service malfunctioned. It was suggested I remove and reinsert the control card which was located on the back of the receiver box. Upon removal, I noticed a number sequence, 15555536. I realize this sounds very scant at this point, however, I am able to, as they say, "only reveal the tip of the iceberg" on the significance at this time. I will say a significant identification number, randomly was assigned to me many years ago, involves 555155356. One may ask, why raise the subject? My reply would be I am keenly aware many people have had similar experiences and they are potential sources of power. Frustratingly, it is untrained power. The thought here is, be encouraged. Stay attuned to it. Do not let it slip away. You must try to harness it.

I watched Olivia as she drove away thinking it would be a cruel part of fate, if I never saw her again. A few days later, I had red roses delivered to her in class. I did not identify myself. I wrote a note on a small card in Chinese characters, phonetically, "wo yao ni xin." Later, I realized it was grammatically incorrect. I should have written "wo yao ni de xin." The translation of what I wrote was "I want you heart'. The "de" would have provided the possessive, "I want your heart." I was a bit embarrassed, but more disappointed because I did not attend that evening, withdrew from the class and never saw or heard from her again. From that day forward, the thoughts of her have intensified, become overwhelming and occupy a great deal of my days and nights. I cannot seem to achieve peace. During the night, I awaken and call her name low and out loud. I pray for her telephone call. No longer can I imagine being without her forever. Always, I am on the lookout for her car. I frequent Vietnamese restaurants in the city and surrounding area where she said she resided. During the past several months, I almost have eaten as much Vietnamese food than in my entire tour of duty in Viet Nam during the seventies. I have grown particularly fond of a special soup which is prepared PHO style. The soup's ingredients are mein, raw and cooked beef, tripe, slowly cooked tendon, sprouts, onion, and other very palatable herbs and spices. Actually, it is the best soup I ever have eaten. I have learned the best locations. Often, I dine at my favorite spot because it is strategically located in the city and the soup at the location is the best. From where I seat myself for either lunch or dinner, I am able to see if she drives by or stops in. Because of cross-cultural appetites, I often visit the large Chinese populated shopping areas, hoping to see her there. From time to time, I follow the rule that one may find the lost person at the location where you last saw them. I sit there on the campus hoping, wanting and waiting for her. I fondly envision our past experiences there. I imagine her appearing and walking toward me with the most beautiful smile I ever have seen. I imagine how she would be attired. Constantly, I long for her. I dream of her visiting my place of employ as she, in the past, indicated she had considered. I constantly think of how I would respond if that were to occur. To begin with, I would be overwhelmed with joy and disbelief. I would speak to her in Mandarin. I would express how much I missed her. How very much I missed her. How much I love her. I would invite her to step forward. I would ask her to wait for me as I concluded the court's business.

I promised to revisit a comment made earlier concerning "love at first sight." I would like to do so at this time. I mentioned "love at first sight" when I first saw her, but I do not really believe in it. One may ask how the two are reconcilable. I believe they are. I did feel love when I saw her. This is because I believe her to be my "eternal companion," "eternal mate" or the more widely used term, "soul mate." I believe we have been together throughout time. I believe we were separated by time, space and memory. I feel, perhaps sometime in the past, I breached our relationship. The breach caused our separation. Our separation is the price I must pay for my wrongdoing. It is my greatest desire to be reconciled with her. I realize life never will be complete without her. So, it felt like *"love at first sight,"* when in fact it was *love all along*.

* * * * *

CHAPTER V

LUNACY OR VISION

* * * * *

Not long ago, I became acquainted with some of the work of Grand Master Liu. Among other talent, he has a special gift in art. He is well-known for Chinese philosophy, deep meditation and divine enlightenment. His paintings are known for their vibrant colors and vivid symbolism. It is said his paintings embody power and the flow of natural energies. One of his publications stated when his paintings are placed in the appropriate direction at the right time and viewed by a person with the appropriate heart, they are known to stimulate energy and induce fulfillment of wealth, love, and happiness. I am particularly fond of two of his paintings "Promotion of Mutual Love" and "Love Forever." My favorite is "Promotion of Mutual Love." This painting may be envisioned only by those with a receiving heart. Its meaning and power will not be revealed without purity of heart. I have come to feel it has certain amplifying qualities and power. It is a water color with vivid emanation. My interpretation of it, and I believe this to be a revelation, is love is attempting to reconcile two former lovers. This is illustrated by a red orb. Their lives are entwined, but there has been estrangement. She gently holds him at bay with one hand, while extending her heart to him with the other. Her heart is held just below his mouth. Happily, but tenaciously, he pursues her. He extends his heart for her to listen and hear, while he gently touches her face. He must speak to her heart as she listens to his. She is very keen to his acts of atonement and is able to discern the truth. The work reveals there will be brighter days for them and a female child should be expected. Almost any price one may pay for the work would be well worth the cost depending upon the viewer's state of heart. Often, I view the work for long periods while listening to a ballad I happened to stumble upon some time ago. It is by John Denver. Let me explain this. I am in the habit of replaying and overplaying my favorites on a disc or other medium. On one occasion, inadvertently, I failed to replay one of my favorite tracts and the next selection began to play. From that day forward, it superceded my favorite selections. I played it 15,556 times. The ballad is entitled: "Lady." Denver, who is another favorite recording artist, deceased as a result of an airplane accident off the coast of California a few years ago. In Lady, Denver asks "... Lady are you happy...are there meanings that you've never seen before?" He sings "Lady....it's like I've never ever loved before." "The day our lives were joined, became entwined...."[25]

Perhaps, communication may be established while listening to the lyrics and contemporaneously viewing the painting with a completely open heart and mind. Could this be possible? Someone believes so. In the painting, consider the lives of the lovers are entwined. She is holding out her heart to hear him and carefully is listening to his heart. Are you getting the sense the author is engaged in fantasia or perhaps suffering some peculiar mental disability? It's like E.T. trying to phone home. "Beam me up Scotty." Why not use smoke signals? Hasn't it occurred to him using the inter-net might be more effective and a lot less time consuming? Perhaps, he is delusional and hallucinating. He may be basing certain life decisions on utter nonsense. What about playing the selection 15,556 times? This is absolute lunacy isn't it? He is a judge? Although never have I been accused of being

[25]

John Denver's Greatest Hits, Volume II. John Denver, perform. RCA Corp, NY. 1983, Number 10.

the brightest, very bright, but not the brightest, among men, I am a very hard worker with a great deal of tenacity. I am fairly well educated and have a great deal of experience dealing with human behavior. Why not explore this for a while to see where the journey may lead us? Assume the playing is symbolic. Equate it to soft water dripping on a hard rock. Assume the selection is four minutes and fifty-two seconds, and a drip occurs every second. The math then is easy. Consider then what happens when the water impacts the rock. One may reasonably conclude, that with time, the water will make some type of impression and eventually will enter the heart of it. As well, the water and the rock had been separate entities. Although not readily visible, each drop necessarily must cause displacement of some portion of the rock and co-mingle with it. The two then flow together.

Returning to music and human behavior, I believe music can cause and affect certain behavior. When coupled with lyrics, it can have a powerful influence on behavior, I believe. Consider Kenny G's "Wedding song." Why was it associated with marriage? How about his selection that causes one to think of love making?

Undoubtedly, you have heard humans use only a small percentage of the brain. People speculate then, what if a larger portion or all of the brain's capacity was utilized? I position that use of additional capacity is unnecessary because humans are accustomed to responding to ordinary stimuli that affect sight, sound, touch, taste and smell. These limitations are placed upon us and to a certain extent, we further them.

A recent article in the N.Y. Times commented on a study conducted by scientists that provided how the brain processes language. The left temporal lobe of the brain is active when English speakers hear the language. Mandarin speakers use the left and right lobes. The right lobe is used to process melody in music. Of course, intonation is very important for effective communication in Mandarin. Master Chi-Jen Liu believes the human brain is capable of having, as he terms, "a third eye." Consider this. If one closes his eyes in darkness, one may envision images. Images are apparent during dreams. The images appear only to be in black and white because we have not trained our brains to draw upon color. What are the images? Likely, they are the result of a perception, usually visual, that the brain has stored. We call the stored data memory. Colors are just more data that are stored. The problem is we have not drawn upon other portions of the brain to store color while awake to envision it with the eyes closed or during dream sleep. Consider you are speaking on the telephone with someone whom you are very familiar and the person is at a place in which you are very familiar. As you converse, from time to time, you envision the person and the place. What if you were speaking with the familiar person while he or she is at a place unknown to you. You only are able to envision the person. What if you are in conversation where neither the person nor place is familiar. Perhaps, you begin to envision the person and place based upon imagination which likely is a result of the persons voice and the purpose for the call.

Certain exercises, eventually, will enable one to envision color. Try this. Close your eyes and envision five buckets of paint. Red, yellow, blue, green and deep purple. Open your eyes and look at separate items that contain these colors. Close your eyes and try to envision the buckets with those colors. Were you able to envision color? Did you experience some visualization of colors while reading the words red, yellow, blue, green and deep purpled which were printed in black on white background? Continue practicing. You may become pleasantly surprised. If you were unable to envision them, try looking at one color. Close your eyes and try to envision the color. Green works well.

Let's shift now to the familiar person at the unfamiliar place. Assume you are unable to find a person you have envisioned. With the proper stimuli, the "third eye" may help you locate the person. Development of the "third eye" may be accomplished by a number of techniques which actually are stimulating the portion of the brain humans normally do not use. The portion is not used because we see no need for it or we do not believe it. Again, we put these limitations upon ourselves.

My mother said when I was a kid, often I would mention events before they happened. I believe this ability now has been clouded by an adult mind and heart. I recall while lying on the couch sometime during the early 1970's and having one of the strangest sensations I ever had experienced. It was sometime during the afternoon. I was awake, but resting. My eyes were open. I felt something happen in my head. I want to be as precise as I can in this description. It felt as if I had been solidly hit like when we played dirt-lot football and I was creamed by some 200 pounder. It seemed I could see stars and felt faint. Or the time I fell from my bicycle onto the pavement without headgear. It was as if I received a severe blow to the head. (Perhaps, this explains my looseness in thought). The sensation was of strong blunt force trauma to the head, however, without the pain. Immediately, I knew something was wrong. I did not know what. I tuned the t.v. There was a news flash. I learned at or near the time of the sensation, singer Jim Croce died in an airplane accident.

If not earlier, some now may be convinced absolutely, this author is a lunatic. The expression that comes to mind is "half a bubble off plumb." Look at it this way. Am I not able to be a lunatic on my own time, if being such does not result in activity that may cause harm to someone else? For sake of argument I am a judge who is insane. Let's say I have the ability to entertain this insanity during my personal time, but to shift to normal, reasonable and well-informed thoughts and cognition during the exercise of my official duties. Should I not be able to do so?

At this time, while on the sanity issue, I wish to revisit the love concept. How is it defined by most conventional thought? Webster's dictionary defines it as "to be fond of, desire." "A deep and tender feeling of affection for or attachment or devotion to," "a strong liking, "etc. [26] I suppose like any other concept, the word associated with it is unimportant, as is the sound created by saying the word unless it is incorporated as nomenclature. Is love energy? Is it a caring adoring form of energy? If so, why not just spell it backward? Evol. Could love be the etiology of the word evolution? Seems logical. I do not like the idea, however, because the sound is too close to the sound evil. So why not spell evil backward? Live. Evil indeed is alive. How about the game of golf? Flog. Now that is interesting. For some reason, when I

[26]

Webster's New World Dictionary, 2d College Edition. Prentice Hall Press. Latest, 1986. Page 838.

would get out on the green, I wanted to call out a different four letter word and it was not "erof," it was "kcuf."

Fromm said "Love produces love." I believe most must agree. Honestly practice and employ its qualities. Allow the practice to become the norm. Likely, you will discover it will produce and/or amplify love in both parties. Synergistically, as Master Liu pointed out.

* * * * *

CHAPTER VI

HOW MUCH DEBT IS OWING

* * * * *

I grew up in a large very Christian family. We were severely warned of the consequences of even considering some other belief may be viable. To summarize, we attended church three to four times per week. We were forbidden to listen to non-Christian music or attend parties. No make-up, haircuts, sleeveless dresses, or open-toed shoes for the women. Fasting until four p.m. each Wednesday. I recall times sitting in school during the late afternoon and being too hungry to concentrate on the subject matter being taught. Occasionally, some of us would fast for three days. Kissing was forbidden and sex was unthinkable for the unmarried.

The early religious upbringing did instill a sense of morals, however. Although, I was one of the poor kids when we lived in the inner city, an environment prone to trouble, my siblings and I always knew where to draw the line. Yes, we threw snowballs at cars and once put excrement on the neighbor's doorknob, but no way did we consider entering someone's home or business, nor did we ever consider intentionally hurting anyone. Frankly, we seemed to come to the aid of someone in trouble. Once I became of age, however, it seems I went wild in the sex area. It seemed I was an unleashed walking hormone. Throughout the years, I keenly was aware life's circumstances could have been worse, nevertheless, often I pondered, why life was so difficult. Was I being punished? I feel certain I did not intentionally cause physical harm to anyone. Clearly, I was not perfect, but it seems I always had a good heart. Then why the suffering? I *bet you dollars to donuts* many of you readers have asked the same question. My second former wife, who was Buddhist, opined I must have committed some major wrong in my previous life.

My reply is, if so, it sure would be nice to know the offense so I could learn therefrom. Could it have been adultery? Please heed this valuable lesson. Under no circumstances should one put down another's faith and beliefs. During the early times with my second former wife, I said something to the effect I am Christian and I do not belief in that Buddha stuff. I do not want the altar in my home. She removed it. It occurred to me then, why is my insignificant self, so holier-than-thou, who hardly is able to make sense of his own circumstances, in such a position to determine what is true and what is not true. After many mishaps in many areas, without going into detail, I decided to rectify my arrogance. I hope I have been successful in doing so.

Christians believe through grace we are forgiven for our sins. If you believe with a repentant heart, you are assured a blanket pardon. It is called "grace." For some reason, especially in the area of promiscuity with women, I did not want the blanket pardon. I asked God to cause me to recall every instance of indiscretion, no matter how long it would take. Upon recollection of the deed, I then would ask to be forgiven for it. I then asked that the event be cast into "the sea of forgotten sins." It took a very very very long time to remember all of the instances. Honestly, I am too embarrassed to say how long. It was painful to dredge it all up. But this is scary. In some cases, I recalled it with pleasure. I then felt compelled to ask to be forgiven for fondly recalling some of them. It was only then did I ask for the blanket pardon. I felt only then could I truly atone. I must say life's circumstances have improved. *If one is expecting to be blessed, he must have faith and the willingness to act upon that faith. It is not faith if "your bets are covered."*

A common thread or underpinning to most religious belief is life hereafter. I suppose some readers here may not believe in life hereafter. I suppose also then they may not believe in life heretofore. If that is in fact the case, I guess all of us are nothing more than energy which ceases to exist for all purposes upon death. I would say the nonbelieiver can be the energy. I will continue to believe I was and will be.

* * * * *

CHAPTER VII

THE SCIENTISTS

* * * * *

Understandably, we place a great deal of confidence in the conclusions of scientists, our brain trusts, often without question. The human being feels comfortable when able to support postulates and hypotheses with scientific confirmatory data. Indeed, scientists have made impressive and significant advances in the life and physical sciences which have promoted the general and specialty aspects of medicine, physiology, psychiatry, physics, communications, engineering and many other disciplines which improved and extended the live span of mankind.

Let's consider, however, other hypotheses which cannot, at least to date, be verified by scientific approaches. This, of course, does not mean they are unworthy of belief. They cannot be disproved. At one time "bleeding" was state of the art medical procedure. Remember the critiques of Pasture, Wilbur and Orville Wright. Edison, Franklin, to name a few. More contemporarily, remember during junior high school science classes the prevailing view "the earth is a closed ecosystem." "There is not one more drop of water or mineral on the earth today than since its forming millions of years ago." I suppose the converse also must have been true. There is not one less drop. The thinking was matter, including water, merely changed form.

Possibly the theory has been modified after man left the earths' atmosphere and landed on the moon, for example. Do you think Neil Armstrong returned to earth with all matter he left with? If he ingested food, he must have eliminated byproducts. Perhaps, it remained in the space craft. Perhaps, it may have been say, just fun, to urinate in space to observe the results. What about the waste containers aboard Apollo II. Were they emptied there? I suppose this is something NASA never would reveal. What about all the stories of space junk? On the closed ecosystem theory, had scientists considered perhaps, vapor could escape once it was in the far reaches of the earth's atmosphere. What do the scientists say about gravity? A force that can cause all matter within the earth's atmosphere to accelerate toward the surface of the earth. I recall a very colorful description of the effects of gravity given by a physics student several years ago. Please consider it from the perspective humor was intended. He pointed out an area on top of his head where he experienced hair loss. He explained the spot was not exclusively the result of hair loss, but gravity at work. That gravity constantly is pulling all living bodies toward the earth from where it originated. To the grave, so to speak. The gravitational pull in his instance, caused the soft tissue of his scalp and face to be drawn downward along with the skull itself. But because the more durable skull was better able to withstand the pull than soft tissue, separation of the hair occurred. He explained gravity is one of the causes of sags under the eyes, cheeks, face, chin, neck, arms, stomach buttocks, legs and other places on the body. That gravity's pull, over time, causes the looseness of the skin. He explained the pull, over a substantial period, is the reason older persons seem to have excess skin. He continued that eventually the force will cause slumped posture, again pulling the body toward the grave. One may become wheelchair bound, then bedridden and non-ambulatory. He continued that while in the bed the pull will cause the skin to adhere to the linen. Eventually, the pull on the now fragile body may so pressure the chest, the lungs cease to function and at that time, gravity has done its job.

Interestingly, gravity's etiology may be from the word "grave." Perhaps, the converse is true. Have scientists considered perhaps it is not an energy from within the earth, but an energy from without. Let's say, for example, forces from beyond the atmosphere cause the earth and the earth's atmosphere to be able to maintain integrity. That all matter within the atmosphere falls to or remains on the earth's surface because of a force pushing from without. The ocean, for example, is held to the earth's surface because of an outer pushing force. If the force no longer pressured the earth, theoretically, the sphere would lose its integrity. The same also would be true of the gravity theory. I only mention the possibilities because, oftentimes strictly held scientific thought and belief becomes questionable or even disproved, as advances are made.

For many years, meditation was considered junk science. Thought on the subject has evolved, however. Recently, Time Magazine featured an article entitled "The Science of Meditation." It discussed the work of Dr. Herbert Benson, MD, who founded the Mind/Body Medical Institute. He conducted very impressive research on the subject. The research concluded that meditators could counteract stress, maintain a healthy body, and achieve a calmer and happier state. "All I've done, is put a biological explanation on techniques people have been utilizing for thousands of years, he said."[27] Experiments demonstrated meditation lowered activity in the parietal lobe. The lobe is a portion of the brain that orients you in space and time. By

[27]

Time Magazine, August 4th, 2003. Page 52. Herbert Benson, MD, Prof. of Medicine, Harvard Medical Sch.

lowering it, one can lose sense of boundaries and feel more "at one" with the universe. Does this mean if it did not function at all one would "feel" no sense of earth's boundaries? If regulated, this could be a good thing.

The article goes on to discuss meditation blocks information from entering the parietal lobe. Scientists are discovering that with enough practice, brain neurons will adapt to direct activity. The discussion, primarily centered on methodology that can cause one portion of the body to impact another. What about a portion of the body, the brain, being able to receive thoughts, ideas, messages from exterior sources through a perception other than the five senses-sight, sound, touch, smell and taste? Most would call it extrasensory perception or ESP. I prefer to call it spiritually guided perception or SGP. As we know, all must agree there must be a source in order for there to be a perception. Say for example, the brain receives a message "do not take that roadway today." The person heeds the message and later determines likely he would have been killed or seriously injured had the message gone unheeded. The question then becomes, from where did the message originate? While I do not know the answer to the question, I, and I am sure many of you readers, have experienced this phenomenon. This is an example of a being's brain receiving a message from some unknown source through other than one of the five senses. Could you consider then, the person being able to send such a message, and if so, to a specified recipient? What if, in the first scenario where the message received from the unknown source is in fact a message from someone who loved or cared for the recipient? Have you ever watched a movie where a seance was held and living beings contacted the dead loved one? We somehow associate this with evil. I am not sure why, but consider, if one is able to send such a message to a deceased loved one, why is he not able to send it to a loved one who is living. Perhaps, the only difference is the loved one who is dead, is listening. It may be reasonable to wonder then, communication to a living loved one is possible through an unknown medium. To be acceptable to the scientific mind, I will analogize my comments to the cell phone principle. Many years ago, one's sanity may have been challenged if he advanced a theory, one day, persons may be able to communicate with others by placing a satellite in space to receive a signal which then is transmitted to a recipient who is on earth, or elsewhere. What if the message that warned of danger might someday be directed to a specific target who is able to receive it through thought processes? Advanced brain development? Let me share this with you. Do you recall my comments about 515, the last digits on Olivia"s plate. 5/5, 5/6 and 3/6 as birth dates, an address, account balance. Etc. Earlier, I mentioned the numbers and combinations thereof have seemed to surprise and plague me over the years. What is the source of those messages? Why have they been revealed over and over throughout the years? Why is this occurring?

* * * * *

CHAPTER VIII

MY OWN TIME

* * * * *

I would like to return again to the sanity issue in an attempt to put it into proper context. I am hopeful no reader will be offended by the degree of cruel detail which must be provided for that purpose. Any day between Monday and Friday, one may visit a courtroom throughout the country and witness cases which involve extreme cruelty and violence firsthand. By law, trials are conducted publicly in public forums.

Let's say that on any given day, I walk into a courtroom during my professional time and hear facts that are as egregious as the following. A mother took her two young daughters, ages six and ten, out trick-or-treating. The three returned home whereupon mom asked the girls to bathe in order to remove their costume make-up. Due to limited resources, it was necessary for the mom to work at night. After the girls began to get undressed, the mother left for her nighttime employment. Unknown to any of them, the defendant was inside the home and hiding in a closet. Once mom was gone, he entered the bathroom, horrifying the girls. He ordered them to continue to get undressed. He sat the 6-year-old on the side of the tub and spread her legs to visually inspect her such as a doctor might do during a female examination. He did the same to the ten-year-old. He then told the ten-year-old "you will do." He tore curtains from the window and bound the six-year-old. He took the ten-year-old from the house and into his car. She also was bound with pieces of curtain. He drove to a remote location and began his sexual assault as follows. He repeatedly raped her vaginally and anally, alternating between the two acts. He tore vaginal and anal tissue as he did so. The youngster was horrified, hysterical and suffered a great deal of pain. The defendant did not care that he was depositing fecal matter into the vaginal area as he continued the assault. This caused super infection. He forced the girl to orally copulate him without first cleaning himself. The child gagged and regurgitated as the defendant ejaculated in her mouth. He continued the conduct over a period of about twelve to fourteen hours. He then tried to sell her to men on the street.

I was in the courtroom and heard the foregoing evidence. During the presentation, as the defendant sat there smirking, my thoughts were, I would like to kill this subhuman now. Before the killing, I would like to inflict corporal punishment upon him with a whip. I personally could carry it out. I realize, however, I am a judge and must honestly and fairly administer justice in the case as in all other cases which may come before the court. I must protect and afford the defendant the substantive and procedural due process rights that are guaranteed by both federal and state constitutions. This is so even if it meant I could not allow the jury to hear certain portions of the evidence or make any other required ruling which may benefit the defendant. I cannot unlawfully disadvantage him in any way.

I must follow the law. I fully recognize I cannot punish the defendant consistent with my thoughts on what an appropriate punishment might be. I am duty bound to follow the law. I took an oath to follow the law. To do otherwise would be evil. I would not perpetuate evil because of evil doing by another. I ask you, am I crazy because I respond to evil in that manner, in thought, on my own time? And yes, it is 'my own time' anytime it does not affect the defendant. Let me also point out that often the thoughts are involuntary. *"My own time" should include the moments when the entertained thoughts are completely irrelevant to any ruling I may make on any matter which may pertain to any issue in the case. Further, it means, not even subliminally, would the defendant be adversely impacted.* I ask you to tell me what punishment would be appropriate under the foregoing set of facts. Before you do, consider that I gave him 935 years of imprisonment. He is inside and has a job. He earns money on this job. Also consider, sometimes weaker inmates are held down so other inmates can continue perverse propensities. Involuntarily, I entertained the thought he should get what he deserves behind the prison walls. I felt like 'dropping a dime on him'. He gets 50% time off for good behavior.

'My own time' in the justice system context is equivalent to my reaction to, for instance, a newspaper article or book that may involve extreme cruelty, callousness and evil. The other day, I completed reading of a book entitled "Falling Leaves" by Adeline Yen Mah. It is a true story of an unwanted Chinese daughter. After reading it, my reaction was a strong desire to be able to fashion punishment and administer justice to every deserving character in the book. Even those who now are deceased.

I suppose certain criminal defense attorneys might say, "this man does not belong on the bench." "How could a person who could entertain such thoughts be a judge?" "The *Draconian* measures he wishes he could impose." "The defendant could be rehabilitated and returned to society." "He is a human being who made a mistake." 'On my own time', my response would be, "I don't care whether or not the defendant could be rehabilitated." "F__k him!" "His rehabilitation is not an issue." "Never should he be returned to society." "He is not a human being." "My sympathies are with the victim, not the defendant." "Her life is a wreck." "Never will she forget the defendant or his sexual assault upon her, whether during the daytime or during nightmares." She always will remember his face and filthy body. As well, "Draconian" is a 'buzz word' which widely is used in the criminal setting." 'On my own time, I say castrate him without anaesthesia'. I think, the questionable sanity characterization would be appropriate if 'on my own time' I did not respond to a defendant's misconduct in some similar fashion.

Olivia, let me mention at this point that as harsh as this discussion is, I am a person with a good compassionate heart and good moral standards. I recognize there are many circumstances when a judge should exercise mercy, compassion and leniency. My natural disposition is to be kind, gentile and loving toward loved ones and kind, courteous and personable to persons, generally. Frankly, how I must respond to evil is the part of me I wish was unnecessary for you to know, but it is my responsibility, a responsibility I cannot forsake. I will say this three times during this writing. *"The height of my love for you Olivia is the depth of my disdain for evil."*

* * * * *

CHAPTER IX

COMPASSION, LENIENCY & MERCY

* * * * *

I am not removed from the realities of the world out there. I've been before the courts when both kindness and injustice were shown to me. An instance of injustice was when, during my late teens, all us boys had hot cars. I was thrown into jail overnight and paid a fine for drag racing. I experienced first hand, as in any group, police officers can be corrupt. In fact, unlike on other occasions, I was not guilty of racing that time. The officers were flat out dishonest. I did stop drag racing, however. An instance of compassion and kindness was shown during college. I found myself hungry and without funds. In desperation, I took food, was caught and appeared in court. The matter was dismissed. Had it not been for someone showing a little kindness, mercy and compassion, the event could have had much worse consequences.

I strongly believe certain experiences shape our fate. It appears my fate is to judge. It is unclear to me for what reason I was destined to judge. I believe certain events, like my personal court experiences, help put human behavior into perspective. Sometimes, I am reminded of those experiences when that young man is standing before the court.

I recognize, for certain cases, compassion, mercy and leniency become indispensable to dispensation of justice. They must not be misplaced, however. They must be exercised when and where appropriate. In the cases heretofore mentioned, I believe any leniency or compassion would be misplaced and irresponsible. In cases involving that degree of severity, I am compelled to and will deal with them in the harshest possible lawful manner. Still not convinced? I will share another real case. At its conclusion, consider your view of an appropriate punishment. You are the judge. The following case is before the court. It involves two men who are cousins. They forced the victim to bend over the back of a couch. They repeatedly raped her. While the sexual assault was taking place, a ligature was tied around her neck and slowly tightened. This continued for several hours, until the victim died of ligature strangulation. *The victim was the mother to one of them and the aunt to the other.* Does castration without anesthesia still seem too barbaric even to entertain the thought 'on your own time'? How about with anesthesia? Should they be given mercy?

Compassion, leniency and mercy suggest they should be exercised when the individual or his circumstances warrant them. However, very often, difficulty lies in determining whether they are warranted. Consider this case. A seventeen-year-old honors high school girl student and her eighteen-year-old boyfriend, a Purdue University engineering student were on summer vacation. Both were excellent students, especially in math and science. They decided to go on a crime spree that summer, however. They were from Taiwan and familiar with the travel habits of many in the American Taiwanese community. They capitalized on that familiarization. Their *modus operandi* was to determine what family returned to Taiwan for an extended stay. The girl then would persuade a locksmith her parents were away and that she locked herself out. The locksmith then would change the lock. After gaining entry, the students resided there and consumed what was available, including use of cars, making international calls, credit cards, cash, etc. Before return of the owner, they moved to the next house. On one occasion, the girl drove a 'borrowed vehicle' and bumped the rear bumper of a car being operated by an elderly woman. After the woman exited her vehicle to assess the situation, the boy jumped into the driver's seat of the woman's vehicle and drove away followed by the girl.

The two were prosecuted separately. The boy received nine years in prison. I was assigned the girl's case. The prosecution wanted seven years. The defense argued her age at the time of the offense, lack of criminal history and exceptional academic performance warranted leniency and a chance at probation. That local jail time, approximately nine months, community service that involved tutoring students without compensation, and full restitution, up front, to the victims were warranted under the circumstances. I was concerned with what would be great disparity in sentencing between the two perpetrators who were similarly situated, the exception being, at eighteen years, the boy was considered an adult. Nevertheless, I decided to show a little leniency. I believed leniency to be the right thing under the circumstances. For several months thereafter, the girl returned to the court and proudly showed her grades, all of which were exceptional, especially in chemistry and mathematics. She showed great progress with the community service. It seemed my decision was correct until approximately a year later. This is what occurred. She and a new boyfriend killed a boy, stuffed his body into the trunk of a car and set it afire. Her reason for the killing was she had stolen money from the victim and he threatened to report it. In turn, she feared returning to court for a probation violation hearing.

Often, the difficulty in assessing the appropriateness of compassion, leniency and mercy in many cases is not knowing the secret thoughts of the criminal mind.

* * * * *

* * * * *

CHAPTER X

THE INJUSTICE OF 'CRUEL & UNUSUAL PUNISHMENT'

* * * * *

I could not resist comment on another constitutionally based fundamental of American Jurisprudence. In my view, it is an excellent example of an area where we have *intellectualized ourselves into oblivion to the extent commonsense has been obscured.* Consider the following case synopses as cases on point. They factually are true, as I recall them. I will not disclose my relationship to them because revelation may tend to indicate the court where I serve. As earlier mentioned, such revelation may run afoul of government regulation.

Case #1: The defendant saw an elderly man parked by the roadside using a two-gallon container to put gasoline into his car. The defendant approached, threatened to kill him, and robbed him. After taking the man's possessions, the defendant severely beat him. He repeatedly kicked the victim while he was on the ground. The defendant then poured gasoline on him and set him afire causing his death.

Case #2: The defendant and his companion kid-napped two young teens from a fast-food hamburger restaurant. The kids were driven to a remote location. The defendant produced a shotgun and, without warning, shot the first child in the head. The child's head disintegrated. Upon observing this, the second child fled out of pure terror. He was caught by the defendant who had him get on his knees to beg for his life. The second child screamed, cried and begged for the defendant not to take is life. The defendant taunted the child in this manner over a period of time. Try to imagine what the child was experiencing. Mercilessly, the defendant discharged the shotgun into the head of this victim. After walking back to the car, the defendant began eating the hamburgers which had belonged to the boys. While he sat there eating, he saw a piece of the second boy's skull and brain tissue on his pants leg. He continued eating, laughed as he flicked it off, and said "I sure blew the little bastard's heads off didn't I."

Case #3: Over a period of months, the defendant and his companion kid-napped young teen girls from the streets of Southern California. After getting a victim into his van, he would tape record the following scenario. The girl was stripped of her clothing. Consider the terror she felt at this point. The defendant and his companion repeatedly vaginally and anally raped her. This not being enough thrill for them, they taunted her with plyers. First, he would pinch a small piece of flesh from her body. Then a larger piece. Seeing this was a thrill, he decided to apply the pliers to her nipples and twist them off. How was she feeling then? He wanted a greater thrill, therefore, while his companion held the victim, he used a pliers and vice-grip to grab her vaginal lips. As he pulled and tore what, obviously is some of the most sensitive tissue of the human anatomy, he would say "scream louder bitch, scream louder." The screaming and suffering of the victims were something most of us could not begin to imagine. Most of the trial jurors could not bear to continue to hear the tape which was produced by the prosecution as part of the evidence. The defendant then raped her again while slowly forcing an ice-pick into her ear and eventually into her brain causing her demise. The defendant cut the word 'whore' into her stomach with a razor blade before throwing her body onto the freeway.

Tell me what is cruel and unusual punishment. I suggest it would be cruel and unusual to cut off the hand of a person who was guilty of theft. To torture an individual who was guilty of robbery or burglary where no victim was injured. But what does the concept mean? In the aforementioned cases, I suggest the defendant set the standard of cruelty. In addition, he set the threshold for what is unusual. If a defendant used pliers on the flesh of the victim, in his mind it was something that was doable. It was not unusual to him. A purely commonsense rule can be applied in these cases. Let's assume the guilt of the accused is not in question. As a judge, I would have no difficulty with cutting the flesh from his body with a whip or causing his castration or both before his execution

It would be very typical for the defense in a case such as these, after all else fails, to produce evidence that the defendant was abused as a child. He was molested and brutalized. The psychiatrist will verify that such treatment would cause the poor defendant's 'acting out'. Typical question to the examining psychiatrist, "how do you know these things happened to the defendant?" Response, "he told me so." "His family told me so."

Such defendants typically use, and I will not overstate this, hundreds of thousands of dollars in attorneys fees, court costs, appeals, and institutional maintenance for more than twenty to thirty years. This is sickening to me. Perhaps, I do have a warped sense of justice.

As a follow up, the defendant in case #3 is still in prison on death row. A few years ago, he sued the Department of Corrections for providing him with broken cookies with his lunch. As ludicrous as this may seem, a federal judge was at least required to read and consider his writ before denial. And yes, the ACLU will continue to thwart his execution.

As a citizen, I am mad. I am damn mad. I have been in the system a long time and, no doubt, *we have our heads up our intellectual buttocks in this area.*

Do you still resist the death penalty? What is your purpose on earth 'as a good man or woman'?

* * * * *

CHAPTER XI

GREEN CARDS
FROM TURTLE EGGS

* * * * *

In the Chinese community, the expression *"turtle egg"* is pejorative. Right down there with filthy, immoral, indecent, corrupt, pond scum. Pond scum probably is a little better because, often it is found on top of water. I laughed when I first heard the expression. My second former wife left it on my voice mail one day. Her accent made it more humorous. She pronounced the word turtle like ter-tul, and as if the syllables were two distinct words. "Turtle egg," "turtle egg," "turtle egg," "I know you are there" she exclaimed. My then teenaged daughter heard it, laughed and said "wooo! That is very scary." Never have I been given a satisfactory explanation why a turtle's egg, in that context, is so repugnant. In that community, the turtle itself is served almost regularly, and if prepared properly is quite palatable.

On a very serious note, the previous chapters pretty much discussed a good man's duty to respond to evil in the judicial context. At this time, I would like to address the duty as a private citizen.

Most would say, would they not, that what truly is evil only can manifest itself through man, and no one person may effectively address all of man's evils. Collectively, however, I believe man's effort could cause dominance of good over evil. Sometimes we characterize individuals who risk personal or professional security for the sake of addressing an evil as heroic and courageous. Nevertheless, there are many instances where mere exposure of evil is all that would be required. For instance, reporting a crime. This chapter is intended as such a report.

How many have seen office signs that advertise "Immigration Services," "Visas," "Passports," etc? They are quite common in coastal and point of entry cities. I would like to comment on what many of these operations are about. Some of these businesses provide legitimate services. However, many do not and cannot. Take the first category, "Immigration Services." What does this mean? What does it imply? I suppose it could mean passport photos are offered there. That the photo could be placed in a neat little booklet and given to the individual to be attached to a passport. What else? Not a lot. If I needed immigration service, meaning that perhaps I am at risk of deportation, would like to become naturalized ("green card"), or need a work permit, the first question I would ask would be 'what is the lawyers name?' If there is no lawyer, I would leave, realizing I could not get much more than a photograph or assistance with filling out a form for an exit visa. Often, you see these operations in predominantly ethnic communities. I will comment on certain operations as they impact Chinese communities because of my familiarity with them in some of those communities. Many operate like this. A person who has overstayed his visa, whether for business, visitor or student, enters the office. He or she is greeted by a receptionist. Usually visible is a handful of typists. The receptionist and typists speak fluent Mandarin, but very broken English. Most of the workers are without legal status. The office cannot assist them. They are in a position to be exploited, typically, they are. They work long hours for peanuts. No benefits are available. Sometimes, sex is demanded. They are completely unprotected. To whom might they complain? Certainly, it would not be law enforcement. How the client is treated often depends on one's gender. Let's begin with the male client. He is greeted by the receptionist in Mandarin. He feels somewhat comfortable in dealing with a fellow countryman. He may or may not be charged for an initial consultation with the "Immigration Specialist." That depends on how timid he may appear. "The specialist," a non-lawyer, typically is also the owner of the operation. He is well versed in American customs and has some knowledge of immigration law and procedures. Typically, he is from mainland China or Taiwan, but has legal status in the United States. He will conduct the initial interview and thereafter, impart the good news that his agency is in a position to solve the immigration problem. Most often, he has no ability to solve the problem whatsoever. To solve it, in the vast majority of cases, a license to practice law would be required. Without the license, I cannot imagine what immigration problem this specialist would be able to solve. The client extensively is interviewed. As much personal data as possible is elicited, whether or not relevant. The specialist will use this information to his advantage and against the client at a later time. The word processors then begin pumping out very impressive looking documentation. Of course the client cannot understand it because all is in English. Of course it must be, because it must be filed with the Immigration and Nationalization Service (Office of Homeland Security), explains "the specialist." Typically, a large deposit is required. This amount varies depending on the information gathered during the interview. It could be ten, fifteen, twenty, fifty thousand USDs or more, depending on what the specialist believes he can get from the client. It has no correlation to any service to be rendered.

Months have gone by and the client has heard nothing except when he telephones the office every few months for a status check. He is put off for as long as possible if "the specialist" believes the client to be unable to provide additional fees. If it is believed the client has additional resources, he is called in with the news. A certain immigration or other American public official wants more money. "He is dishonest, but what can we do?" says "the specialist." A refund would be impossible at this point with all he has vested to date, which is very little. The additional amount being demanded, again, is anyone's guess. Often it is whimsical. If the second sum is given, the client is put off for several more months with the assurance that all is now going well and as planned. In actuality, nothing is happening except delay and grand theft.

How long can this go on? One might ask. For as long as possible. When delay no longer seems possible, that magic day arrives. The "Green card" has arrived and is available to be picked up at the office. The excited client is overcome with joy and excitement, he may even tip the great "Immigration Specialist." The happy client goes on his merry way and proudly uses and displays his green card. That is until he attempts to use it for government services, say at the department of motor vehicles, social security office, enroll in school or travel outside the country. If the agency checks. The now distraught client learns for the first time, the card is invalid. That's right phoney-baloney. He is lucky if he is not detained on the spot. He returns to the office of the "Immigration Specialist" to find the office has closed with no contact information. The client cries out or thinks to himself of "the specialist," "ni shi chou wamba dan," translation, *"you dirty stinking turtle egg."* In the meantime, the turtle egg has opened an office at a different location waiting for the next Chinese national.

Earlier, I mentioned how the client is treated, often depended on gender. If you are a young female, look out. Be prepared to be propositioned for a lot more than USDs. Why not call the police? Think about it. The "turtle egg" is driving around in his shiny new S-Class Mercedes. He is well-to-do. Often, connected. Sometimes he has access to members of Asian gangs. They can be quite intimidating if paid enough money. Sometimes, the eggs scratch the backs of one another. The "turtle egg" has all the client's personal information. He knows where to find him.

So there you have it. The "turtle egg" continues preying upon the victim who cannot report it to the police for fear of deportation. The bottom line for the Chinese or other national, *no matter what promise or representation may be made, "never will you get your green card from a turtle egg."*

* * * * *

CHAPTER XII

THE GREEN
HAT

* * * * *

My first marriage occurred when we were very young and, no doubt about it, very immature. Like most young couples, our best friends were another married couple. They married even at younger ages. The four of us spent a great deal of time together and I always will fondly carry those memories. In time, our friends had two children within two years apart. Things seemed to be going well. However, one day, my friend, the husband, revealed he was having an affair. I was not particularly concerned. I figured it would go away and not be a problem. It did not. He began to spend more and more time away from home. We tried to dissuade him from continuing the liaison. Finally, he moved from the family home. I witnessed his wife transform from a happy vibrant beautiful young woman to almost a catatonic existence. Into a state of complete despair. These events occurred during my graduate school days. During the six months following their separation, sometimes, I would drop by and bring milk and pampers for the children. I recall times when the refrigerator almost was barren. Sometimes, during very cold days and nights, heat was unavailable because the furnace fell into disrepair. I would use a portion of my student loan proceeds to help her out a little. Sometimes, she was so distraught, I would comfort her with talks and assurances things would change. I was there on a regular basis. I truly believed the consoling to be helpful. Soon thereafter, however, I discovered I was having feelings toward her I knew I should not have. I was not trying to overreach her during this very vulnerable period of her life. She was my friend. I felt a great deal of sorrow for her as I watched her suffer for so long. I wanted to help her. I could sense her feelings toward me were changing. Eventually, it became a stand-off which neither one of us knew what should be done next. It was bittersweet. In time the issue was over. I stepped outside the bounds of my marriage and, of course, her union no longer existed. Times seemed happy and sad. My wife completely was unaware. First there was guilt by both of us which then turned into deception. We began to plot how I could see her more often. Upon learning, my wife was, what I would say, devastated by the news. To fully appreciate this, I must note I was the first man ever in her life. It seemed I had become her life. She trusted me. After digesting the news, she became physically ill. She began to remain in bed most of the time. She became fearful and irritated when I would leave the home, even for reasons known to her to be legitimate. I tried to repair it. But as time revealed, it did not work. She left me. After completing graduate school, we attempted reconciliation. We spent years together, but it was of no use. The horrible indiscretion, and I consider that characterization a euphemism, rocked the whole basis of our relationship. It just could not survive. The marriage ended in a dissolution.

In his materials on the subject, Master Jen Liu pointed out that astrological charts warned of adultery and that ancient and present adulteries were due to astrological incompatibility. I suppose he meant the two of us, for whatever reason, should not have been together. I am not sure on this point. Likely, in this case, it means I was unworthy of her.

Years thereafter, I met my second wife who was Buddhist. She strongly believed whatever improper conduct one may have been involved in, he or she, in turn, would become the target of the misconduct. I found her to be very interesting. She added another dimension to my life by introducing me to, what I believe to be, the very misunderstood Chinese culture, a culture well worth getting to know. An area of misunderstanding for instance, is in America there is a commonly held belief that Chinese people tend to be unfriendly. I believe the reason for the seemingly unfriendly outward impression is, in Chinese society, emotions such as warmth and affection, ordinarily are not publicly displayed. It is not customary for the citizenry to greet one another while in public places. I recall walking on some of the main thoroughfares while in Beijing, Shanghai and other cities. Upon greeting persons from time-to-time, some continued to look straight ahead without a response while others responded. In each instance there seemed to be surprise that I addressed them. In some instances, it was apparent never had they seen a person who was not of Asian descent. I was amusing to some of them. I suspect, in many instances, people from homogeneous societies, learn racial bigotry only after leaving their country.

Once becoming acquainted with most Chinese people, one would find personable traits to be in abundance. My in-laws were very kind, warm, gracious and caring people. I gleaned this the instant I met them. Some on them never had met 'a foreigner'. I had an instant family with whom I became attached during my first visit to China.

I began to enjoy "the real" Chinese food. Not only did I enjoy eating it, but also, I enjoyed the manner and the reasoning behind its preparation. Many of the customs were fascinating. I began to learn the Chinese communities and study the Mandarin language, the official language of the mainland. I enjoyed visits to the cities that are famous for tea and silk. Touring many of those areas involved wall-to-wall people, shops, boutiques and fast food-stands which emitted pleasing aromas. Some offered foodstuffs, never before had I seen. It seems always, I have had an open mind while participating in new dining experiences and those occasions were no exception. Tradition dictates that a large feast with very exotic foods be served on an occasion such as my travel to China to meet my in-laws for the first time. The feast lived up to tradition. I was informed thereafter that some of the dishes I very much enjoyed, included meat from the horse, dog and snake.

When we first met, my second wife seemed to have a great deal of genuine energy toward me. However, after a year or so, trouble loomed on the horizon and soon thereafter, hit us full-throttle. The union was headed for disaster. She was insecure about my first wife. She became physically aggressive. It seemed the aggression had no end. Often, I found myself having to make excuses for my bruises. I was not without fault, of course, but violence was unacceptable. One day after months of attempting to resolve the issues, I found she caused me "to wear the green hat." Many of the Chinese readers know what is meant here. For those who are unfamiliar with the culture, further discussion may lead to clues to the meaning. If not, it may cause you to seek out a Chinese person for elucidation of the meaning. It may be fun to meet someone new.

My second wife had been unaware of the specific reasons for the breaking of the marriage to my first wife. She had been unaware of my misconduct. I would like to take a moment to reflect on the adultery subject. When it occurs, how does it hurt? It hurts one's ego, senses of respect and self esteem. The deception itself is devastating. How could the person who was to be so close, possibly commit such a betrayal? One imagines what happened between the two adulterers. It is mental anguish you cannot escape. You demand an explanation. Why? You demand to know the detail even though the detail will cause much more pain and anxiety. Nevertheless, you insist. As you suspect the detail is given in less than a full accounting, you experience anger to the nth degree. You insist not all is being told. More surfaces which compounds the problem. More lies are told. "Yes, it happened many times." "No, it only happened a few times." "No, it only happened once." "No, it did not happen at all." "Yes, it happened, but only once." More coverup occurs. You still cannot imagine the person being desirous of the other over you. If you become intimate again, during sex, you envision the two adulterers. A mishmash of fact and imagination grind away at you. The ghosts in your mind haunt you day and night and you find you cannot eat or sleep. It is difficult to function on the job. Even your free time is excruciating. *You begin to feel the same mental anguish and pain you inflicted upon another.* Your body becomes weak and fatigued. You become physically sick. To you, the relationship is over. You now feel you owe the person no allegiance. None. One may have to come to terms with the realization the injury was so great it cannot be repaired. It is something I never again would inflict upon another.

* * * * *

CHAPTER XIII

DEPRESSION & DISGUISED
OPPORTUNITIES

* * * * *

The bottom line of prevailing theories on the causes of depression is either it is physiologically or environmentally caused or a combination of the two. For example, a chemical imbalance or a saddening/tragic event/ circumstance or both. Those who suffer depression, appreciate it in varying degrees. Adultery could be one of those triggering events. My first inclination was to keep the following information private. However, I have decided to disclose it. Later, I will comment on my reason for the disclosure.

Throughout the years, I recall depression being ever present in my life. I attempted to battle it without professional intervention for most of my adult life. The practitioner's diagnosis-enzyme imbalance. However, on occasion "the state of things" or "a triggering event" caused deep or extreme depression to such a degree that self destruction not only was contemplated, but attempted. On one such occasion, after passing out, I guess that was what it was, I recall being in an emergency room. I could hear a great deal of commotion. I could feel my body being worked on. Most of the time, it sounded as if I was hearing it all from a distance. At some point, I realized I was watching the emergency team at work on my body as it lay on the table as I stood beside them. I then lost consciousness, I guess. The next I recall was waking in a recovery room. Later, I was informed that during the procedure, my heart ceased to function. For those who may believe this not to be credible, my response would be "I was there and I experienced it." Let me share that although I continued to experience depression until meeting Olivia, I was able to put an end to the madness of attempting self destruction. I believe very strongly we become acquainted with certain people for a specific purpose, even though such purpose is not or never becomes apparent. I believe meeting my second former wife, the Buddhist, was for such a purpose. She imparted that had I been successful at self-destruction, I would be returned to earth. The notion solidly hit home. My feeling being there is a possibility of truth to the assertion. The drastic destructive steps never again were contemplated.

As I mentioned earlier, after meeting Olivia, whether or not I see her here on this earth ever again, the depression is 100 percent gone. What if I never had met her during this lifetime?

Although I was reticent to offer advice on the subject, I believe my insight and experience may provide a useful perspective. My advice would be, in addition to professional help if it is available, suffer the difficult circumstances until they change or until your time here on earth is over. You do not want to leave here due to an artificial reason intentionally caused by you. For doubters and nonbelievers in the possibility of reincarnation or similar beliefs, let me make inquiries and observations. Actually, there are very few possibilities here. Do you believe someday you will die? If so, do you believe you would cease to exist for all purposes forever? If so, would you agree then you were nothing more than a form of energy? Do you believe anything survives the body after its death? If you believe something survives after death, you must believe it exists someplace, don't you?

Perhaps, some readers believe, at this point, among other things, the author to be imprudent, indiscrete, and deeply troubled. Earlier in time, some of those descriptions may have been appropriate by those who never had experienced chronic acute depression.

One may be puzzled. Why a fairly intelligent well-educated person would divulge such information? Indeed, the privacy concern was an important consideration. However, after a great deal of thought and balancing the potential benefit which may be derived from disclosure with possible personal ramifications and concerns, I chose disclosure. It occurred to me *how often is one able to share a message, possibly with the world that, at least, has the potential to benefit mankind, even if in small numbers.* Consider the number of people worldwide who suffer varying degrees of depression and those who were successful at self destruction. Especially so in many eastern societies where self destruction under certain situations is widespread and sometimes expected or encouraged. The young student who fell a little short on a critical qualifying examination, for example. Let me share with the student, likely, the circumstances of going forward with the examination were created by someone else who made demands on you for differing motives or they were created by you at their behest. I say "forget it." Prepare heartily. Be prepared as well as you can be. Read the questions, ponder them, think. Then 'puke your intellectual guts all over the paper.' But once you have exhausted all possibilities toward your endeavor, move on. You are destined to do something else. Perhaps, your falling short was an apparent adverse circumstance but, in fact, *a disguised opportunity or an opportunity turned around.* I recall being faced with a similar circumstance. I fell short on an important examination. Although feeling devastated at the time, the failure caused me to shift to other possibilities. Today, I feel certain I would not have been able to achieve my present position had I been successful on that examination. Frankly, success on the exam would have had a limiting impact on my career. It seems I am destined to do what I am doing.

Some time ago, after serving on a lower court for five years, I resigned and took a job elsewhere in the country. It was believed the states' U.S. Senator would nominate me for judge of the federal district court in that area, and thereafter, former President George H. W. Bush would appoint me to the position. What I did not count on was George H. W. losing the election. Needless to say, I was taken aback. I hightailed it back to my home state, got lucky and was appointed to a higher court than where previously I had served. The point is, had I been appointed to the federal court as envisioned, likely, I would be there now. *Surely, I would not be where I am 'finding Olivia'.* On the idea of *foregoing an opportunity which would or could produce good if acted upon,* throughout the years as I experienced what I believed to be good workable ideas, often I allowed them to remain dormant. A good example of life in quiet desperation. I realize now, had I acted upon some of them, it would have been beneficial or at least productive of good. Do you recall when last you were presented with such an opportunity? Did you act upon it? In the instance with Olivia, I refused to let it slip by. I told her why. I am certain that meeting her *again* caused me to spring to life many ideas which likely would have remained ideas. Since meeting her this time, I receive a constant confluence of thoughts and ideas I believe are worthy of, at least, memorializing. Something has prompted me to write about them. I am uncertain of what and why. What is it about meeting her that would prompt writing a book? What is it about meeting her that would cause introspection of my purpose? I do not consider myself a writer. Perhaps, you do not either. I met her, and after losing contact with her, the thoughts began to flow. It seems during every night and day, since meeting her, I cannot achieve rest until I make some type of notation of those thoughts. Could it be that writing is the medium which should be used 'to find' her? What if she happened upon a copy? Don't want to flatter myself, but what if she is trying 'to find' me?

For those who are in an environment that seems to dictate hopelessness or helplessness due to inadequate financial resources, access to educational and employment opportunities, etc., my advice is *address the circumstances within the boundaries of the law and good morals.* This is your proving ground. A true test of your character. You must not 'check out' and risk the possibility of return.

On the disguised or opportunity turned around idea, keep in mind when one elects, partakes or involves oneself in any undertaking, necessarily, another has been foregone. Consider this. Do you recall when I had red roses sent to Olivia? Sure I was disappointed that I did not hear from her thereafter. As it turns out, indeed, it was one of the disguised opportunities. What if I had heard from her at that time? Certainly, I would not have written "Finding Olivia."

* * * * *

CHAPTER XIV

SUICIDE, SEX & SPIRITUAL MATES
(SOUL MATES)

* * * * *

I prefer use of the term spiritual mate over soul mate only because it seems use of soul mate is like flagellating the deceased equine. I could use them interchangeably, however. The concept is the same.

Earlier when I mentioned one of the consequences for suicide would be a return trip to earth, I failed to mention that under Buddhist doctrine, one could be returned seven times. Each time being with increasingly difficult circumstances. Each possibly resulting in suicide. If the seventh opportunity does so, one would be forever lost. My former second wife opined I am here on my seventh time. I suppose her position cannot be disproved. One observation I could make is, as earlier mentioned, I often pondered why, throughout the years, life's circumstances seemed to be so difficult. Without detailing, it seems I endured adverse physical and mental circumstances from childhood until relatively recently. Perhaps this is the answer to those earlier ponders.

On the subject of sex and soul mates, Christian doctrine teaches that if one breached the commitment, in effect, the breaching party caused his or her mate to experience the conduct engaged in by him or her. For instance, all the sexual acts committed by the breaching party, caused his spiritual or soul mate to have engaged in those same acts with the other person. This may explain why the conduct is so destructive to the aggrieved party's psyche.

Many Buddhists believe upon the instance of death, the spirit or soul would occupy another body, human or otherwise depending upon one's historical behavior. I do not necessarily disagree. However, it would seem as logical, in that way of thought, upon death the spirit would be held in abeyance somewhere at a place unknown. At some point, either instantly or much later, it would occupy a body. I mention this because people have a tendency to place a great deal of weight on age and age differences for pairing purposes. If you are spiritually connected mates, for the most part, the age differences are immaterial. For discussion, consider for example, Olivia and I are spiritual mates. We became estranged. Our bodies deceased at different times. Assume I was required to return to earth much earlier than Olivia to create a significant age difference to advantage her in our new relationship. Can you appreciate the invaluable lesson I have learned or should have learned? I must now find a way back to her under the new circumstances. Suppose again Olivia and I are spiritual mates. At some earlier time, I breached our fidelity commitment and we became estranged. Consider the earlier scenario that after the two of us deceased, I returned earlier in time and we now are at the present point where I have undertaken the search and am seeking recognition by her. Perhaps, but consider a slightly different scenario. What if after the occasion where I breached our commitment, Olivia committed suicide. What if the two of us now are here for a return trip. Olivia mentioned that others say she does not smile enough. What motivates a smile? Generally, happiness. What if she is in a state where there is not a lot to smile about. Perhaps she is generally unhappy. What if her unhappiness is because she cannot determine her purpose. What if she chronically feels the incompleteness spoken of earlier. What if she is looking for her soul or spiritual mate, but does not recognize him. Perhaps, her life is incomplete because of the absence of her mate, whether or not she realizes it. *I must find her and cause her to recognize me no matter how I have been disguised.*

* * * * *

* * * * *

CHAPTER XV

THREE WIVES

* * * * *

Master Liu wrote of frivolous love and "changing spouses like underwear."Notwithstanding, his point is not incongruous with religious and societal teachings that provide adultery is an acceptable reason to dissolve a union. Perhaps one should, if maintaining it would become more destructive. An option might be to buckle down and ride out the physical and mental sickness associated with the storm. At this point, both your mind and body likely have been seriously injured. The body will attempt to repair itself, including the emotional injury. Over time, the pain will lessen and the ghosts and boogie men in the mind will seem less threatening. Let me make a point very clear. I am not attempting to advocate how one should resolve this very serious difficulty. It must be dealt with on an individual basis. Only the injured individual would be able to take corrective measures. This is one reason why the injury is so great. The injured party is in it alone. No matter how well intentioned family, friends, healthcare practitioners and others may be in attempting to guide and heal, the victim must make the critically important decision.

Few would deny human sexuality is nearly as great a human behavioral need for overall well-being as eating and sleeping. Long-term starvation, eventually would lead to death. Long-term sleep deprivation could lead to severe abnormal mental and physical conditions which could prompt and promote self destruction. Long-term sex deprivation, in most people, may lead to abnormal behavior, physical and mental anguish as well. If widespread, lack of procreation would result in extinction of the species. Why then is such a moral premium put on human sexual behavior? The main and most obvious reasons are the accomplishment of sex usually involves two people, while eating and sleeping behavior do not. As well, sex between two people, most often, is the ultimate intimate act toward commitment. Commitment is important for species pairing. Pairing is necessary to maintain an orderly society of a species.

Perhaps, I broke my commitment with Olivia during a previous life. *Perhaps she wore the green hat at that time.* More than the humiliation, I cannot imagine hurting her. Although there is karma between us, she no longer fully recognizes me because of the misdeed. Master Liu might say we would not have met and became entangled to the degree we did, had there been no previous significant relationship or contact of some sort. It seems clear she is cognizant of something about me. She is not sure of what it is. I believe she does not fully understand why she approached me for the first time. I wonder, would I be able to persuade her, and to cause her to 'recognize' me? Publicly, I will wear the green hat in an attempt to break the causal chain. I hope when I see her, if I see her on this earth, she will be donning a pink hat. For many months now, I have tried to find Olivia. I suppose I will continue to do so for many more months or perhaps years to come. I will continue searching the Vietnamese and Chinese populated areas. The markets, food courts, restaurants, bookstores, and anywhere I believe there is the slightest possibility I may find her. *The major difference in trying to find Olivia this time is, from this day forward, I will search those areas while visibly "wearing the green hat."*

Consider, had I not been made "to wear the hat," however. Likely, I would not have met Olivia again. As it turns out, *"having to wear it is one of those disguised opportunities or one turned around."* I need her in my life for completeness. I pray eventually she will 'recognize' me. I pray for full reconciliation. I must contemplate, however, if she does not, that I will bide my time on earth without her. I will continue to accomplish my mission here, but always look forward to seeing her.

During the last several years, I have become more spiritually guided. The guidance has intensified since meeting Olivia again. My mind seems more open and receptive to the uncertainties which lie ahead. As such, I become joyous at the prospect of finding her and, of course, saddened when I consider I may not find her. When I mention "finding Olivia," I mean it in a much broader sense than being in her physical presence. It encompasses also, her recognition of me. Recognition in the sense that she fully appreciates who I am, and if so, is she willing to or has she forgiven me. Once I asked of her religious beliefs to which she responded she was unsure of them. This suggested her open-mindedness on the subject.

When I contemplate the remainder of my life with Olivia, I feel complete. I feel whole. I feel completely at peace with myself. Life just could not be better under that proposal. When I contemplate life with her, my grief and sorrow no longer are present and I do not fear life's trepidations. The fact of the matter is, when you meet your eternal, spiritual or soul mate, it is something you just know. Returning to Elton John's lyrics *"the second that the hammer hits."* This is what I experienced upon seeing Olivia again. One may ask three questions at this point. "How are you so certain Olivia is your spiritual or soul mate?" How are you certain former wife #one is not?" What about former wife #two? How might you be certain she is not?" These are very legitimate inquiries. As earlier mentioned, former wife #one was a person of high moral character. I was her first and without fault by her, I damaged our relationship. To this day I feel indebted to her. It seems to be a wrong I cannot correct. If a rectifying opportunity presented itself, I would act on it. Reflecting back when we made the decision to marry, I was in another state and in the company of a childhood friend. Although former wife #one and I had maintained a romantic relationship for some time, I mentioned to my friend I was feeling uncertainty in proceeding with the marriage. I felt something was missing. We were very young at the time and he tried to give me assurance it would be fine. I merely was experiencing as it is said "cold feet." At the time, he had been married for a couple of years. I persuaded myself to return home and proceed with the ceremony. Thereafter, I continued to experience the sense of incompleteness. No doubt, she could have done much better than marrying me. She was entitled to be in a complete union. She was pure at heart and very beautiful in appearance, mind and spirit. Finally, it was revealed also she experienced incompleteness in our relationship. Perhaps it was because of my misconduct. Perhaps, her incompleteness was for a reason only known to her. If she has not, I hope and pray she will find her eternal mate very soon.

Regarding former wife #two, let me digress just a bit to again raise Master Jen-Liu's warning of changing mates like underwear. Causing one "to wear the green hat" is sufficient reason itself to dissolve a union. Due to the suffering it caused and the damage continuing it could cause, I did not see a healthy, happy household. My heart now is gone. The union was destined to dissolve. I came to this realization before my reintroduction to Olivia.

Again, I will impart my belief that people sometimes are destined to meet for specific purposes. I believe former wife #two was destined successfully to immigrate to the United States. Concomitant with that destiny, she was to bring Buddhist messages. She delivered one that rang loud and clear to me *"self destruction would lead to return to earth to suffer greater adversity."* The message had a profound impact on my life. I believe, as well, our meeting was to expose her to Christianity which she discovered has many parallels to Buddhism. Always, I will have a special place in my heart for her as the mother of two of my children, whom I love very much, and for being the emissary for important insight.

If I am fortunate enough to find Olivia, one thing is certain, it would not be analogous to discarded underwear or any other garment. *She is my "Lady" and life, whether or not I ever again see her on earth.* I am prepared to be her armor. A helmet to protect her head. Strong and durable to perform the task, yet light enough for her to wear comfortably and with ease. A robe to wrap her body. Strong to protect her, yet provide softness and give sufficient space to enable her to stand alone. Her boots to protect her feet. Strong and durable and provide a solid foundation for us, yet give her liberty to walk unimpeded. Some time ago, I was moved by the words of Kahlil Gibran "Love one another, but make not a bond of love." "Let it rather be a moving sea between the shore of your souls."[28] I would wisely use my experience to enhance her intellect to go forward in meeting the challenges of life. As earlier mentioned, Dr. Cutler posited that our purpose here is to achieve happiness. I recognized once here, we desire and pursue happiness. Nevertheless, I believe we have individual purposes. I believed my purpose was to fight evil. I realize now that seeking happiness is a consequence of being here and fighting evil is such a consequence and duty for good men. I agree with Master Liu's observation "...our true purpose in life is to find balance in giving and receiving love."[29] The observation is consistent with the realization *my true purpose on earth is "Finding Olivia."*

28

The Prophet Kahlil Gibran, Author. Alfred Knopf Pub.
17th printing, 1988. 1st pub. 9/1923. Page 15.

29

Chi-Jen Liu. Page 13.

* * * * *

CHAPTER XVI

WHY 'FIND OLIVIA'
THE "THREE MEANINGS?"

* * * * *

Let's examine the components of the name Olivia. Symbolically, perceive the 'O' as a circle. Once completed, a circle is continuous without end. The circle then signifies 'always or forever'. Liv means 'to live'. Via means 'by way of'. To be meaningful, the two must be supported by the common 'v' yielding, 'live by way of'. Combined, the name Olivia means "always or forever live by way of." What does this mean? Let's refer back to the "three meanings." (1) "Evil flourishes when good men do nothing." [30](2) "The mass of men lead lives of quiet desperation"[31]and (3) "Love is the active concern for the life and the growth for that which we love."[32] The three concepts are interdependent. Assume 'love' to be atop a pyramid because of its significance in human life. Assume a good man's duty of "evil abatement" is placed at opposing vertexes and "quiet desperation" at the others. The dynamics are, if one truly loved or sought love, necessarily, it must actively be pursued. Implicit in pursuit is one may not live in quiet desperation. If one does so, he would be without love. As well, one cannot abate evil if he is in a state of quiet desperation. Love is diametrically opposed to evil. Conversely, evil is diametrically opposed to love. Only good men will attempt to abate evil. Only good men can love. The concepts are mutually interdependent. Must not one agree

30

Burke

31

Thoreau

32

Fromm

then that *"Olivia" suggests a never-ending obligation to live by "the three meanings?"*

After having read sixteen chapters, you may think "this is interesting stuff, maybe you don't, but where is the story of Olivia as was promised?" I have had enough theory, philosophy, invective and spewing of venom as well. Do you recall the portion of "An Overview" where "the three meanings" as they relate to purpose, love, sex, happiness depression and suicide will race the story to an unexpected and dramatic conclusion? I am ready to jump right into it. However, before we get there, I would like to honor certain commitments I made earlier during this writing. It will be very brief. It will not exceed five pages. I promise. I will entitle the chapter "Loose Ends & Old Lovers."

* * * * *

CHAPTER XVII

LOOSE ENDS & OLD LOVERS

* * * * *

The only reason I decided to entitle this chapter "Loose Ends & Old Lovers" is because it reminded me of a George Strait tune from one of his greatest hits compact discs. The tune was "All My Ex'es Live in Texas."[33]

Do you recall different times during this writing, I indicated I would get back to a particular topic later or explain something later? For instance, *leniency mercy & compassion, love at first sight, Olivia's absence from my life, the meaning of 'finding' Olivia.* I believe I did so. There is one area, however, I believe, where there was no closure. It was when the lovers of old were willing and, indeed did, suffer or die for the loved one. I indicated my willingness to do the same for Olivia. I then pointed out the self-serving nature of such an assertion, and yada! yada! yada! or yeah! yeah! yeah! Lofty words. Perhaps, never to be tested or acted upon. Knowing the inadequacy of one option, I said "if not true, then so be it." Thereafter, I attempted to prove the assertions to be true. I want to make one additional attempt to solidify the offering. Let's take the most serious "I would be willing to die for her." First, one must assume a scenario. One of us must die. Then assume I would have the option of making the decision. With that, look at this perspective. If I chose life over hers, where would I be? I would be here without her. My purpose here is to 'find' her. I believe under that scenario, never would I have even the opportunity to 'find' her *again*. However, if I chose her life here on earth and forfeited mine, I would be "*somewhere*," wouldn't I? Wherever that may be, I would be waiting her

---

33

MCA, Universal City, CA. Copyright, 1987.

arrival. Her arrival would be inevitable, would it not? The first option would have such an ephemeral result would it not? A few meaningless years remaining upon this earth without her and without ever again having the possibility of 'finding' her. I am in it for the long haul. Life here without her would be insignificant. One may be reminded of the self destruction discussion. One may say "you don't care much about life anyway, what would be your real loss?" My reply would be self destruction only was possible during her absence from my life. It related to a period of time before meeting her *again*. After meeting her *again*, whether or not I 'find' her this time, I have a clearly defined purpose now, *"Finding Olivia."*

* * * * *

CHAPTER XVIII

DREAMS
COME TRUE

* * * * *

Several months have passed since last seeing Olivia. However, my thoughts of her have intensified. It seems nearly twenty-four hours per day. I think of her. I see her in my minds eye, I want to touch her and constantly, I long for her. Last night, after arriving home from work, I decided to take a little rest. Without getting undressed, I lay on the bed looking at the ceiling and, of course, contemplating Olivia. I closed my eyes. I was at rest and it seemed I was nearly asleep. My mind was very active, however, because Olivia was still there. I always envision her as she appeared during our last meeting and how much I want to see and be with her. As I had done on so many prior occasions, I spoke her name aloud, then lowly and softly. I thought, enough of this imagination and hocus-pocus stuff. What concrete steps might I take to find her? Likely, she no longer is a student at the college. I returned there so many times to scour the campus for her as often as I could. When we last spoke, she mentioned she would be continuing her education at a certain university. I went there on several occasions to find her as often as I could. I do not have her sir name. I did not have an address or a telephone number for her. For kicks, I decided to dial the number our former fellow classmate had given to me several months ago, even though it was not in service at that time. The idea came to mind after recalling it as lyrics in a song by Garth Brooks "What She's Doing Now." After a couple of rings, as I was expecting the "no longer in service" chime and message, I was surprised by a female voice who answered. Reluctantly, and with a great deal of nervousness, I said "may I speak with Olivia, please?" The voice responded "this is Olivia."

I became so euphorically debilitated, I hardly knew what to say and even if I did, it would not come out right. After pausing for several seconds, the voice inquired "who is calling?"

I had to say something and, in a really squeaky voice, I managed to get out "this is Tristin."

She said, "wow, how did you get my number?"

I responded "do you remember when I asked our former classmate for it after you missed several classes?" "At that time, it was not in service."

She responded "I do recall that." "It temporarily was out of service."

Without further thought, I said "Olivia, I must see you."

Reluctantly, she gave a long "okay." "When?"

I said "how about now?"

Again, reluctantly she said "okay, where would you like to meet?"

I responded "Border's bookstore, or there is a quiet lounge at the Hilton in your area."

She responded "although I rarely drink alcoholic beverages, tonight, I think I will have a glass of wine." "The quiet lounge would be fine." "How about in 45 minutes?"

I said, "I will be there waiting."

At that point, I was beside myself. I hardly could wait to hang up the phone. "Oh God!" "Oh God!" "Oh God!" "What am I going to do?" I rushed into the bathroom, brushed my teeth, gargled. I jumped into the shower. I couldn't wait for the water to warm. It was cold and I kept dropping the soap. The sprinkler system kicked on and caused the water pressure to drop. I was in too big of a hurry to wait. I got the soap off as best I could. I cut my face while shaving and could not get the bleeding to stop. As I was attempting to put bathroom tissue on it as a stopgap, I lost control of the roll and it began to unroll onto the floor. Quickly, I tried to re-roll it without success. As I ran back into my room to dress, the tissue was stuck to the heel of my foot and left a long streamer behind me. It seemed all was going wrong. My big toe poked through a hole in one of my socks as I pulled it on. I pulled if off and frantically searched the sock drawer for another suitable pair. I nearly ripped my pants while hopping on one foot and trying to get the other one into the other pants leg. I fell to the floor. I got up, put on a pullover and ran down the stairway and out to my car. I thought "is it clean enough?" "Nothing I can do about it now," I thought as I continued to pull my belt through the loops. As I accelerated away, I thought, "better slow down, you will be further delayed if stopped." I tried hard to compose myself as I parked and quickly walked toward the lobby. I was a few minutes early and found a restroom to further primp. "I look terrible," I thought. "Look at this hair," "look at this face." I tried different expressions, smiles, postures, poses and voices. I was not pleased with any of them. "Come on Tristin, be mature, calm down," "she's just a baby," I said to myself. I tried to appear confident and stood with my back straight as I walked into the lounge area. There she was as beautiful as ever. It seemed my heart pumped almost violently as I approached her. I tried so hard to hide my anxiety. It appeared as if she had lost a little weight since last seeing her. I toned down comments which would have expressed what I felt in my heart, "baby you are so so beautiful," "I love you with all my heart and soul" to "Olivia, you look great." "Looks like you have lost a little weight." She said "it's good to see you again Tristin."

In my nervousness, I said "can I drink you a buy?" Then I said, "what I mean is, can I buy you a drink?"[34] The transposition was there because I heard the inquiry many times on an old George Strait CD and somehow it stayed with me. I did not intend to use it at that time. It just came out that way. We began to get reacquainted as we sat there sipping white wine. I just could not keep my eyes off of her. The most beautiful woman I have met in my entire life. She wore a pink soft mohair top which more than complemented her petite, but well sculpted body. Her knee-length skirt, which featured a brief slit on each side, fit so superbly. It nearly drove me out of my mind. I got a scent of her perfume. It was so so sweet. I noticed her slippers which partially revealed her delicate feet. I wanted to skip all the preliminaries and get right to the act of holding her. I sat across from her to enable me to get a constant and unobstructed view of her. No table or other furnishing interfered with that purpose. I looked at her face, hair, eyes, neck, arms, delicate hands, and all else I could take in without being too obvious. As the wine began to have a calming affect on me, the evening progressed wonderfully. But almost out of nowhere, Olivia said "Tristin, I kept my distance from you after the night you told me of "the three meanings."

I wondered "why?"

---

[34]

George Strait, Best of. 1987. "The Chair". MCA Records. Universal City, CA.

She said "do you remember the night I returned to class after being sick?" "As it turned out, I have a terminal illness." "As fond as I was of you at that time and continue to be, I thought, what is the point."

I jumped to my feet and it seemed as if I pulled her up along with me. I grabbed her and held her tightly. I closed my eyes and said "dear God, oh no, not Olivia, please not Olivia." "Please not Olivia." "Oh God, no." "Not Olivia." "Please not Olivia." I began profusely to sweat. My shirt became wet with perspiration. I said "no, not Olivia." "No!" "No!" "No!" At that time, I opened my eyes and continued to scream "oh God no." "Please, not Olivia." I then realized I was in my bed and only had fallen asleep.

As I sat there, it occurred to me, my longing for her had begun to hurt. I had become very stressed. I thought, get a grip. Life on this earth for you must go on until your time is up, with or without her. You already have reconciled yourself to accept either possibility. With that thought, I decided to get up and go out for a late dinner. I thought, why not have dinner, you know where, in the Vietnamese/Chinese community. I drove to one of my favorite restaurants. As usual, I curiously was recognized with a smile by the owner. He had come to know me by sight and it seems, at times, he almost expects me. I sat at my usual table and ordered the large bowl of soup, PHO style, that I have become so fond of. I decided to treat myself to a Tai-tea as well. Dinner was great and I was very relaxed as I sat there thereafter and pondered Olivia.

I left the restaurant and was returning home when I saw a "Border's" bookstore. The sight immediately brought to mind a presentation given by Olivia during our class. During the presentation, she mentioned how she enjoyed the store because light snacks and beverages were available while she browsed, read or studied there. During the presentation, she was casually attired with a pastel top and light or beige corduroy pants. It appeared as if she was wearing 'cowgirl' boots. She stood tall and erect. Her hair was styled with long loose waves which reached her lower back. Her face was excited and aglow. She was confident, but soft as she addressed us in Mandarin.

I was favorably impressed with her skills in that area. Of course, almost all in attendance were native Mandarin speakers. One may ask, why are students whose native language is Mandarin enrolled in a Mandarin Chinese course? What occurs, I believe, is the young students realize that an easy "A" could be earned to boost the g.p.a. Olivia, however, honestly desired the course to improve her written and verbal communication skills in Mandarin, her native language being Vietnamese.

With a great deal of difficulty, I tried hard to follow and understand the words she spoke. One reason for my absolute attention to the subject matter was I wanted to find out more about her. A reason for the difficulty was, although my Mandarin skills were appropriate for that level, the class was moving at a much more rapid pace because of the fluency level. The professor believed I would benefit from that level of intensity. I must say I did, indeed, benefit therefrom. Another reason for my difficulty during Olivia's presentation was, flat out, the intensity of her beauty. It was as if I now had a valid reason to look at her uninterrupted. In the past, I suppose, I appeared strange by the number of times I looked in the direction of her desk. My eyes were glued to her during the presentation. You should have witnessed her delicate gesturing and soft angelic voice all of which touched my heart. I could not help but watch her every step as she returned to her seat.

On a whim, I decided to drop in the "Border's." My thought was to have a latte, perhaps. I like it extra hot, no foam. During undergraduate and graduate schools, I suppose I was a coffee addict because it seemed no amount of caffeine, day or night, would interfere with my sleep. Embarrassingly, I will say during that time, I would consume up to fifteen cups of coffee per day. This night, I did not feel like sleeping anyway.

I scanned the combination bookstore-café as I entered. As I headed toward the menu, I noticed a young lady who was seated to my right. She appeared to be reading a book. At that time, I only could see the side and back portion of her body. She seemed a little taller than average, nevertheless, petite with beautiful soft brown hair with just a little curl to it. A more precise description would be loose falling wavy tresses. After placing my order, I stood there waiting its preparation. The area was not very large so the young woman easily was noticeable. As she shifted in her chair, I began to see more of a profile of her. At that time, I believed I wanted Olivia so very badly, my mind was playing tricks on me. I began to believe the young lady resembled Olivia. The hair, shape of the head and the small portion of the side of her face I could see, all seemed consistent with Olivia's characteristics. I paid for and received my purchase and began to walk to a seat that would provide a better view. As I did, she turned and looked directly at me. Oh my God! It was Olivia. I could not believe it. My heart began to race. I hardly could breathe. I thought, "what if I begin to hyperventilate?" I tried hard to compose myself, but to no avail. At that point, everything seemed to begin moving in slow motion. I must have bumped something, because I felt the hot latte running down my pants. I spilled at least a third of it, if not more. The heat of it on my hand caused me to drop the mug. The mug shattered. The attendant looked at me in a sympathetic way as I acknowledged her. She then gestured, like, "don't worry about it. I'll take care of it." My attention then immediately was redrawn to Olivia who now was standing and watching me with a wide comforting and understanding smile. We began to approach one another. The tension mounted. Words would not come from my mouth. I tried to say "Olivia. I missed you." I wanted to say "Olivia. I love you." "That some time ago, you touched my heart, but now you have captured it." Before I could utter virtually anything comprehensible, she extended her delicate hand and gently placed her index finger on my lips signifying no words from me were necessary. She said, in the softest but clear voice, "Tristin, I missed you." "Tristin, I love you." "It seems so long ago when you told me of the three meanings." "They have changed my life." At that time, I noticed Fromm's "The Art of Loving" lying on the table near where she had been seated. Surely, I had died and gone to heaven or somewhere and about to enjoy life thereafter.

My eyes blurred a bit with, what I believe, was light moisture from the emotion of the moment. I was completely stunned. I was relieved and happy. No, I was ecstatic. I was overwhelmed with myriads and myriads of emotions. My knees felt weak. She readily realized my distress and extended her arm as if to direct me to a seat. I did not want to sit at that time. All I wanted to do was to hold her. I thought. Here is the love of my natural and eternal life. Hoping I would not offend her. I went for it. As I reached for her, she extended her arms in a welcoming manner. Finally, after all the difficult and grievous years without her, I was in a state of bliss. I could feel the blood rushing through my veins and arteries. I now could feel the warmth of her body. To my surprise, I could feel the rapid beating of her heart and slight trembling of her body. Her smile turned into a look of contentment. I pressed a little more firmly against her and she reciprocated. This cannot be true. How often in life do you get exactly what you want and pray for. I was completely blown away and I sensed she knew it, because she looked at me as if indicating everything was okay.

* * * * *

I suspect Olivia and I stood there in silence for 15 minutes or more, oblivious to our surroundings. Finally, I tried to speak again. I was able to whisper to her saying " Olivia, I love you more than you can imagine." "Never again do I want to be away from you." I would have continued but she began whispering to me. She said "Tristin, I know the extent and depth of your love for me and I feel the same for you." I pulled back from her just a little. I wanted to see her face. Was this real? As I did, I could see that her eyes were wet. I knew she was speaking from her heart.

The evening reminded me of the notion *sometimes the longer we wait or long for the object of our longing, the sweeter the unification.* This evening was far more extraordinary and complete than I ever could have imagined. Olivia and I closed down Border's as we enjoyed the company of one another. Where did the time go? We did not want to part company. We were determined to continue at another location.

We thought it would be enjoyable and meaningful to return to the campus where we first met. It was dark, but we felt very secure as we held hands while walking through the common areas. We seemed to prefer silence most of the time. At one point, we decided to lie on the grass. I retrieved a picnic canvas I had in the trunk of my car because of the dampness of the lawn. It was approaching one o'clock a.m. as we lay there in silence looking up at the stars. The night was still and comfortably cool. We would break the silence from time to time to reassure one another we were, in fact, where we wanted to be more than any other place. She then mentioned she was aware I was unable to locate her and on countless occasions, she had been extremely tempted to drive to my workplace. At that point, I began to think of the countless times I imagined her walking through the double doors of the courtroom. What I would say. What I would do. Would it be during a time when it would be inappropriate or difficult to take a recess? Would I be able to remain focused on court business? Olivia began to explain it was traditional in the Vietnamese and Chinese communities for daughters to remain living with the parents until marriage irrespective of the daughter's age. She mentioned even-though she had become, 'Americanized', as they say, she deeply respected their wishes and traditions. She said during the time we were in attendance of the Chinese course, she began to speak of me to her parents. The more she revealed, the more inquisitive and concerned they became. The greatest concern, I believe, was our age difference. I am many years older than Olivia. She pointed out to them, however, that her dad was as many years older than her mother. "That is different!", they exclaimed. Finally, it seemed they forbade her from seeing me. Although disheartened, she acceded to their wishes.

We remained on the campus oblivious of time until the dawning hour. At about 5:15, I knew I needed to get showered and off to work. She realized this as well and let me know that soon we would be together again. We returned to our cars, hand-in-hand. Upon arrival we turned and faced one another. I could see the excitement of the moment in her eyes. I am almost certain she was wondering at that time whether I would kiss her. Oh how badly I desired to. Her lips were thin and cherry red. Her eyes indicated I would be welcomed. As I stepped toward her, I extended my arms embraced her and decided I would savor those precious moments. I would wait for that first kiss until perhaps the next time I saw her. Already, we assured each other never again would we be apart, and only our responsibilities would intervene between visits. We slowly relinquished the hold we had on the hand of one another. I opened her door and watched her place the safety belt into position. Again, we acknowledged very soon we would be together again. I stood there and watched her taillights as they faded into the early morning mist.

* * * * *

The next several hours were almost like a blur. I barely could recall making it home, showering or driving to work. I arrived early, as usual. I prepared the day's calendar the day before. I booted my computer, and began sipping coffee. I tried to turn my attention to the first page of the morning newspaper or as one would phonetically say in Chinese, the bao zhir (newspaper), the "zh" taking on a "j" sound.   It just would not work. I had no concentration or comprehension whatsoever. I gave up and decided to lie down on the couch until first calendar call which usually began at 9:00. I turned off the lights, and appreciated that, I could lay there undistracted and reflect upon the glorious time I had with Olivia. I replayed the drama over and over until I dozed off to sleep.   At about quarter of nine, I awakened from a very restful sleep. I guess the sleeplessness of the past was caused by tension attributable to not having Olivia in my life. I mouth-washed, brushed my teeth again and primped as I looked in the mirror. I began to wonder how such a beautiful goddess possibly could have an interest in me, let alone love me. The thought was ephemeral, however, as I experienced a feeling about her that unequivocally led to the conclusion she truly loved me.

Once I began to undertake my judicial responsibilities, I seemed to be mechanical and distracted. Because of the importance of my work, however, I readily realized it would be a disservice if I did not get focused. By the end of the first session, some of the staff and attorneys expressed "judge you sure are in a great mood today, what has happened?" I replied only "today is indeed a wonderful day."

Throughout the day I would think of Olivia. My thoughts were joyous and I am certain, a smile would come to my face from time to time.

It was nearing late in the afternoon session that Friday. I began to contemplate the evening. When would I hear from her? I did not ask for her telephone number. Certainly, I would see her again. At that time, the double doors opened and to my relief it was Olivia. This was the day I imagined on hundreds of previous occasions. During those occasions, almost every time the doors would open, it would draw my attention. As she hesitatingly entered, I used my eyes to encourage her. I wanted her to feel completely relaxed. Only one brief miscellaneous matter remained on calendar. I wished, somewhat, something a little more substantial required resolution. I decided to extend a little privacy by addressing her in Chinese. It did not appear other Chinese language speakers were present. I said "qing deng yi deng wo." "Qing, zuo." The phonetic spelling is called "pinyin." Pronounced "peen-yeen." The translation of the words I communicated to her is "please wait for me," please have a seat." I wanted to be more eloquent, but my Mandarin speaking skills still were rudimentary. I then returned my attention to the parties before the court. They seemed somewhat impressed.

I was delighted Olivia would be able to observe me in my work domain, acting in my official capacity, yet not involved in a lengthy tedious matter. I thought I would articulate and perform at my best. From time to time, I glanced at her and realized she was watching me in an approving and adoring way. As dreamed on many occasions, heretofore, after the court's business was concluded, I gently motioned her to step forward. I again spoke to her in Mandarin. I said "Qing jin, qing guo lai" which means please enter, please come here. As she approached, all eyes were on this beautiful woman who had come to see me. They watched   as we left the courtroom for the chambers area. Once in chambers, she seemed quite surprised and impressed by my space. She said "you are such an important man."

I replied "I put my pants on and take out the trash like anyone else."

She seemed pleased as I reached out to hug her. She readily reciprocated.

Anxiously, we planned the evening, which in my mind, included a romantic dinner. I thought we might have a glass of wine, thereafter, if she cared to. We had a wonderful dinner. We decided on a restaurant called "Inn of the Seventh" which is located in a canyon area. I suggested it, although never had I been there. She hoped I would make the choice. The reason for my suggestion was my friend Iras raved about it on numerous occasions. She told me how romantic the canyon setting is. That a small brook flowing nearby is especially romantic and enjoyable for outside diners. My friend absolutely was right about the restaurant. It was almost as I had envisioned, and it seemed to be the perfect spot for Olivia and me to become more reacquainted. In my mind, it did not matter where we were, so long as I was with her. I could sense she felt the same. After a relaxing, delectable, and romantic dinner by candlelight, we realized neither of us had consumed a great deal. We were ready for the next part of the evening. We chose dancing. I found a great place that was playing many love songs. I seated myself next to her and we began sipping white wine. She seemed truly to enjoy the moment. She placed her hand into mine. Needless to say, I was delighted. After about fifteen minutes, to my surprise, Celine Deon's "Power of Love" began to play. This was the perfect opportunity to ask her to dance. It would be our first real dance together, being the hundred other times we danced were in my head. As I held her tender hand and led her to the dance floor, I could feel the excitement in the two of us. As I gently placed my other hand around her waist, and moved closer to her, we began to move with the tempo. The lighting was appropriately subdued, but I could see unequivocal love in her eyes. I realized at that time, Olivia truly loved me. Things could not have been better as she held firmly onto me and gently caressed the back of my neck at the hair line. Chills ran down my back and arms. I realized my life here on this earth could not be better because at that very moment in time, at that very place, I was with the person I desired to be with more than any other person in this world. I cannot underscore how much love I had for her.

As the evening drew close to an end, I drove Olivia to her car which had been left at my home. She entered her car as I realized I must allow her to leave. She then asked whether I would like to sit in her car for a while. Excitedly, I took her up on the offer. Once inside, I felt happy to know I would be with her even if just for a few more moments. Seeming to be apologetic, for reasons unknown to me, she said "Tristin, I shared how I feel about you." "I hope you do not misunderstand me, but at this time, I am ready for you to kiss me." Because it was so unexpected, I was completely blown away. My heart was racing, my blood began rushing, honestly, I felt a little faint. Perhaps, many of you are thinking. This man has a real problem. But please consider, however, if you were at that precise moment in time, at an exact location, with the very person you desired to be with more than any other person in the world, you had not seen the person for several months, did not know whether or not you ever would see the person again, having never kissed the person and he or she said "I am ready for you to kiss me." I looked into her beautiful caring and welcoming eyes. As I drew close, her lips were trembling. For the first time ever our lips and mouths met. I held her while leaning over the console as she reached to touch my face. With a slightly, open mouth, she gave me the best kiss I ever had experienced. The sweetness, softness, tenderness, meaningfulness and warmth were electrifying. It was breathtaking. After about a minute our mouths parted. We looked at one another in disbelief. She said "Tristin. I will carry this first kiss with me for the rest of my life." "I would like for you to go inside and get some rest now." "We will see each other very soon." As I exited her car, I almost stumbled because of being overcome with emotion. I had to regain my balance by touching the side of my car. As I watched her taillights fade into the dark, I felt a warmth and caring toward her which I never had felt for another human being.

I reentered my car and turned to a love song just to reflect for a few minutes before going inside. As I began to ponder Olivia, I knew at that moment, one day she would be my wife. I must have fallen asleep, because the next thing I remember was hearing soft music coming from my clock radio which was on the night stand. I turned over and looked at it. It read 5:15 which is my wake-up time. I was fully clothed and realized I had not left for a late dinner the previous evening after all.

* * * * *

* * * * *

CHAPTER XIX

FOUND, FORGIVEN, FORGOTTEN &
REMEMBERED.

* * * * *

Although it was Saturday morning and I could have slept in, I could not sleep any more after that dream. I decided to get up, jump into the shower to clear my head and go out for an early coffee and newspaper. It was nearly seven by the time I put the paper aside. I wasn't very interested in it anyway. My concentration was poor. The dream continued to plague me. At about 7:30, I decided to get another cup of coffee to go. I drove to the campus and, as I had done on many Saturday and Sunday mornings in the past, I sat on the monumental rock in the area where I last saw Olivia. After several hours there, I began to feel weary in my mind. I drove around a little and basically wasted the day.

As late afternoon approached, I thought, "I think I will go to an Asian singles party tonight." My friend goes quite often and always he reported a great time. In the past, I had always declined his prompting for me to go along with him. Tonight, I thought, "why not." "This could be an opportunity to try my Mandarin in a social setting where I would not be acquainted with anyone in attendance." "Why not, I cannot find Olivia." "Am I not just wasting my time?" After returning home, I put on a little music. I won't tell you what it was. It sure seemed to put me in a strange mood. I had two glasses of wine while getting ready. I thought, "I will get over Olivia because I must." I began to lose confidence in what I had strongly believed. "Have I been deceived by my own crazy thinking?" I thought. I'm still in pretty good shape because of regular attendance at the gym and I selected clothing I thought would at least conservatively highlight my best parts. I was not worried about breaking the laws of driving while under the influence of alcohol. (Caveat, the following only is for fictional purposes and should not be relied upon in an attempt to determine whether one may safely operate a motor vehicle). In my early days as a prosecutor, based upon hearing criminalists testify many times, I was aware of certain science. In general terms, 1 eight ounce glass of wine = 1 ounce shot of 86 proof alcohol = 1 twelve ounce can of beer= .02 blood alcohol level. Of course, this would vary depending upon the % of alcohol of the wine and beer. In addition, there are other variables such as food content of stomach, time of consumption, whether one was of average height and weight, health, etc. Generally, I knew it would not be chemically possible to exceed .04 for my body weight and height. The legal limit is .08. As well, even if I was under the limit, if I felt impaired or that I might endanger another, I would not operate a vehicle.

Upon arrival, I discovered there was a good turnout. Still being troubled by the dream, I headed for the bar for a glass of wine. I then had another. I enjoyed sitting at my table watching others on the dance floor and the scenery in general. I noticed a young lady who seemed to be looking at me, but every time I looked in her direction, she looked away. Finally, she smiled at me. Nice music was playing and I decided to ask her for a dance. Thought I would try my Mandarin by saying "Qing, wo gen ni tiao wu ba?" She replied "what was that?" Egyptian?" It means "may the two of us dance please." Once we were on the dance floor, she said "I was sitting there wondering why such a good-looking man would not come over and ask me to dance."

I said "I was wondering the same thing." "Where did he go?"

I then said "it seemed you were looking in my direction, but when I would turn to look at you, you would turn away." "As I pretended to turn away again, I saw you look in my direction again." "For a while, I thought either you were shaking your head no in advance of me asking you to dance or our heads were connected by a pulley." She was pretty cute. As it turned out, we had a good time dancing together.

Several hours later, the party began to thin out. It was time to leave. I thought I would ask for her telephone number and again try to impress her with my Mandarin skills. I said "Qing, gei wo ni de dianhua hao." "Ming tian, wo da dianhua gei ni." She laughed and said "what did you say?"

I then asked her in English "may I have your telephone number, please." "Tomorrow I will call you."

She said "no, but you may take me for a bite to eat." I was surprised, but accepted the proposal. After eating, she said she felt like another glass of wine. It was getting late and being unfamiliar with the area, I did not have any ideas. She then suggested we see her apartment and have a drink there. The earlier dream about Olivia still was kind of nagging me and I felt like going home. Nevertheless, I said "great." Once we arrived, we had a couple of drinks. I was still within the legal limit, however. (Fiction only), as a general rule, under the scenario above, one is able to 'burn-off' up to .075 per hour. What this means is that in about two hours, one possibly could eliminate 1½ glasses of wine). She put on music and sat next to me on the couch. We talked until we ran out of things to say. The conversation between us had gotten pretty loose and probably inappropriate for a first meeting. I told her of the bad experience with my ex. She told me of hers. I kind of knew what was coming. I kind of wanted to and I kind of didn't. Nevertheless, we began kissing. It started getting heavy. She indicated she would hop into the shower. A few minutes later, she reappeared and was wrapped in a towel. She handed me a green towel and pointed in the direction of the shower. I went in, turned on the water and then just sat on the edge of the tub. Strong thoughts of Olivia came to me. At that point, I knew I did not want to continue, and even if I did, I thought it would not be fair to her. I turned off the shower and reentered the room fully clothed. She seemed perplexed and inquired "why?" I said I just did not believe it would be the right thing to do. She stood up and said "ok, no problem." "Good night." She then folded the towel, in thirds, lengthwise. She wrapped it around my head like a turban. I left it there and said "good night." I drove home while still wearing the thing. I went inside and fell asleep. Although my thoughts returned to Olivia, it seemed I fell asleep almost immediately. I guess the wine was enough to cause me to sleep until about nine that morning. I got up, showered and prepared to go out for breakfast. I saw the green towel from the night before. It was clear to me what I had to do at that time. I cut it down and re-formed it into the turban hat. I used my heavy duty stapler and thread to secure it. I put it on my head and walked out of the house. During breakfast, I got very quizzical looks.

I believe I mentioned earlier, I started writing this book several months ago for no apparent reason. Every night or early morning, I almost felt compelled to scribble notes and type out my complete thoughts the next morning. This morning, I felt I needed to include that last dream.

After completing what I wanted to say in the writing, I decided to go to the shopping mall to get a black patch for my name to be embroidered on it. I found one of those small island-type booths and had the name "Tristin" embroidered on it with red thread. I asked the assistant to sew the patch onto the green turban hat. It looked very ridiculous. Nevertheless, I knew what had to be done. After donning the hat, I drove over to the Chinese commercial retail area which, by now, was bustling with people. I parked my car and walked inside the very busy supermarket. Many heads turned at one time or another. There were some laughs and some frowns. I didn't care. I was upset at the loss of Olivia. A strong feeling then came over me that one day soon, I would find her.

It seems not sooner than I felt that, I saw her. She was as beautiful as ever as she pushed her shopping cart, seemingly in my direction. Ordinarily, I would have panicked and gone berserk, but this time, even after not having seen her for so long, I experienced a strange calm. As she approached, our eyes met. She said "Tristin, is that you?" "Do you remember me?"

I said "of course I do Olivia."

I stood there in almost complete silence as I looked at her. It was as if I was somehow tranced. I knew, however, that my feelings for her were as strong as ever and more. I loved her to no end. I was of the impression she was a little embarrassed as I stood there in the humiliating green hat. I knew I had to do it, however. I loved her more than life itself. After a few moments of standing there feeling partly awkward, but completely at ease with her, I handed her the writing I thought was time to call a manuscript. She asked "what is it?"

I replied, "may I not say at this time Olivia." Although I wanted forever to be in her company, and I believed, one day I would, I turned and walked away. As I neared the exit, I removed the green hat and deposited it into the trash. As I drove away, I felt a sudden lifting of what seemed to be a tremendous burden from my heart and mind. *The height of my love for Olivia is the depth of my disdain for evil.*

* * * * *

CHAPTER XX

OLIVIA

* * * * *

A publisher said the manuscript for "Finding Olivia, The Book/The Letters" had the potential for becoming a good seller. He said, perhaps even a best seller. Who knows, it could even make Oprah's book club. I was flattered, but I thought, how many dreams do publishers plant. I truly wanted publication, however, in order to share it with the world. I met a very talented young artist from Berkeley California whose name was Ninjakun. He designed the book's cover. I was very pleased with the final product. The design depicts a judge posed as the famous "Thinker" sculpture by Auguste Rodin. Standing behind is a young Vietnamese woman who, in a comforting manner, has placed her hand on the "Thinker's" shoulder while holding a tulip blossom with the other. At the risk of being cliche, "a picture is worth a thousand words."

After making arrangements with a publisher and advertising agency, advertisements began to appear on billboards, buses, bookstore windows, newspapers and magazines. A tee-shirt also was produced. All the ads read "Finding Olivia, The Book/ The Letters Coming Soon." Actually, I thought some of the ads were very cute. People began to wonder what all the hoopla was about. I had been waiting in great anticipation since seeing the first advertisements. Some were on large billboards located at intersections on major thoroughfares which ran through the heart of the Chinese and Vietnamese commercial areas. They read "Finding Olivia, The Book/The Letters Coming Soon." Finally, after weeks of pre-introduction, I learned deliveries of the book had been made. It would be available on the shelves of major bookstore chains tomorrow morning.

I had been lying in bed since about 8:00 o' clock that evening. I just could not fall asleep. I thought "I cannot go on, I just can't." Every day and night had been a struggle. Constantly, I am filled with anguish. "I just cannot go on alone." I thought, perhaps a glass of wine would help me to fall asleep. The sedatives my doctor prescribed did not seem to be helping enough. I sat there and finished two glasses of wine while listening to soft music, including, "Lady." "One more glass of wine," I thought. I have not achieved deep restful sleep in many days. More and more, I felt as if my sanity was being challenged. I felt so alone. Another glass of wine and I returned to bed. I closed my eyes. I reflected on the good times, the great times, the beautiful times when we were together. I began to sob uncontrollably. I lay on my back, turned to my side, then the other side, then shifted to my stomach. I just could not get comfortable enough to fall asleep. I was so hurt. I just could not bear the pain. I cannot go on without my sweet love, my spiritual mate. As "Lady" played, I screamed out "you are not here beside me!" "I cannot close my eyes and rest my weary mind." At 11:00, not having been able to sleep, I got up for another glass of wine. I asked "why am I suffering this unbearable pain?" At that time, I removed one of the firearms from the safe. I placed it on the table before me. I looked at it as I continued to consume the wine. Because of the rapidity of its drinking, it began to leave an acidic aftertaste on my tongue. Again, I picked up the gun. I placed it back on the table. "What about the sedatives?" "I had 120 pills. Coupled with the alcohol, that would do the job." I decided to open another bottle of wine. I went down to the cellar. Already, I had too much to drink. I never had that large a volume of alcohol in my system before. I missed my footing on the last few steps and fell a short distance to the floor below. I could feel blood running from my nose and mouth. I lay there on the floor for several minutes before picking myself up and returning upstairs. The music was so beautiful. It brought back all the wonderful memories. I again sat at the table and placed a wet soft cloth to my nose and lips. The bleeding subsided. A little wine remained from the first bottle, which I began to sip. "Life here is just too difficult to go on." I lifted the gun. I then considered how my skull would fracture if the projectile impacted my head. Destruction of bone, blood and tissue. I would not want my sweet baby to learn how I died." "I cannot leave her alone in this world." "I love her with all I have." "She needs me more now than ever." I placed the gun back onto the table. I opened the sedative bottle. Again, I began to cry uncontrollably. I put down the pills. I said "This is just not fair. The pain is so great." I then began to ponder the notion that if I did destroy the life I was given, I must return under circumstances much worse than what I had experienced. No! No! No! No! No! "I cannot." "I must tough it out." "I must muster enough strength to survive for her." "I promised my sweet spiritual mate I would and with all my heart I shall."

The next morning should have been the beginning of an exciting day. I felt melancholy, however. It was gray and pouring down rain. As I drove to work, I put on Denver's "Lady" for perhaps the millionth time. I knew I had so much to live for, but for some reason, I continued to feel like giving up on life. I was an emotional wreck. Denver's "Lady" reminded me of "the three meanings" and seemed to reinforce my sadness. He sang of closing your eyes and resting your mind. Of promising to stay forever. The beginning of life together. The lyrics asked for whom tears belonged. Implying them to be unnecessary because of being as close as one can be. They rang over and over in my head as tears began to stream down my face. I thought, "I must get a grip," "it is over, forget about it." I arrived at work early and was able to compose myself to the extent I believed my emotional state was not too apparent. I struggled through the workday and finally, it was over.

After work, it still was raining. I began driving to a "Borders" to see if, in fact, the books were being stocked. The Denver CD still was selected and set on "repeat" for the "Lady" tract as I had left it this morning. The lyrics were there again. But right at the time of playing "the meanings" portion, there was a dazzling sunburst followed by a beautiful rainbow. The scene seemed to comfort me and warm my heart as I parked and walked toward the store. As I stood outside for a while to enjoy it through its duration, I felt as if someone had given me a hug and was holding me. I looked back and no one was in close proximity of where I was standing. It then seemed as if I heard a whisper "You are not alone." Instantly, I felt relief, joy and contentment.

As I entered the store, to my surprise, I saw an entire section filled with"Finding Olivia, The Book/The Letters." Some patrons were lined up to purchase copies. Others were sitting at tables and reading it over coffee. I still felt strangely different and I did not know why. I decided to pick up a copy, purchase a "latte" and enjoy browsing the book there at the store while I watched the customers. This was my first view of it as a completed book. As I opened it and began reading the preface, the words were more meaningful. As I continued reading, I began to laugh. I then felt very serious and I became engrossed. I noticed the bookstore had become crowded with persons, such as me, reading it while having coffee and snacks. I could hear emotions being expressed. Sounds of laughter, at times, disgust, disbelief, "ridiculous!", "wow!",etc. At one point, I observed teary eyes on a number of people. I continued reading. After experiencing a whole panoply of emotions myself, again, I began to cry. I then realized my crying had become very audible. No longer could I control myself. All the wonderful memories of our lives began rushing in. Within a minute or two, people walked over to me and said "what is wrong young lady," "it's only a book." I looked up and said "I am so very sorry." "Hello. My name is Olivia, Olivia Dawei."

* * * * *

CHAPTER XXI

THE RECONCILIATION
& OLIVIA'S LETTER

* * * * *

Never will I forget the day when I was doing grocery shopping for my parents. I went to the Chinese market because it carries many of the items needed for preparation of some of our everyday meals and the Vietnamese markets in the area are sometimes limited in supplies. I decided to shop the largest market in the area. It seems always to be busy and robust with shoppers.

As I browsed, I noticed an American man who was some distance away. What was curious about him was he was wearing a strange looking turban-like hat. Moreover, it was green. I felt certain he was unaware of the hat's significance in the Chinese community. As I continued my shopping, I noticed the man did not have a shopping cart and appeared just to be looking around. I was about to pass by him, and as I did, he looked at me with wide and excited eyes. It was Tristin from my Chinese class. He stood there looking strong and handsome, but I could sense a nervousness he tried very hard to control. I said "Tristin." "Do you remember me?" He responded "of course I do, Olivia." I began to think of those days in class. It seemed so long ago. Tristin seemed so sophisticated and debonaire, but so mysterious, at that time. He also, seemed to be a wealth of knowledge. I remember finding it difficult to look at him for long periods. I suppose he was intimidating to most, but I always could see a kindness, a gentleness in his eyes. I knew he was fond of me back then. Frankly, I knew he had a great deal of fondness for me. Back then, as we began to become more acquainted, I felt he was a little strange, but nevertheless, um..., I would say, I found him to be very adorable. Although he was several years older, for some reason, I felt an attraction, some type of closeness to him. I did not know why.

I recall one night when he wanted to speak with me. I was a little reluctant and had ideas of perhaps, "play it a little cool" came to mind. But my desire overcame my reluctance. He seemed so experienced and enlightening he had me captivated. I would say "Mesmerized." I remember not knowing how to respond when he told me of "three meanings." How they guided his life and made up "his fabric." He overwhelmed me that night, but I allowed him to walk me to my car. Through my rearview mirror, I could see him standing there watching as I drove away. I thought, a good man, a strange and mysterious man.

During one class, fifteen red roses arrived. When the delivery man entered, all eyes, including mine, were on him. With the exception of myself, another student and Tristin, all the other students were just beyond highschool age. Everyone was curious as he walked over to the professor and said "these are for Olivia." My heart stopped, it seemed. All eyes now were glued on me. There was all the reaction one would have expected from that age group. It seemed, the professor wanted to alleviate the pressure on me by calling the class back to order. My hands were shaking as I opened the small attached envelope. Although, I was very nervous, I managed to read the little greeting card which made me laugh. In Chinese it said "I want you heart." I looked up to see if Tristin had arrived. He had not. For some reason, I had a feeling I would not be seeing him again. My feeling turned out to be partially correct. We found he had withdrawn from the class.

I was a little apprehensive when taking the flowers home because my parents asked me not to see Tristin again. We had many discussions of him and the subject matter now was closed. When I entered, my parents looked at one another and then to me. Without a word from them, I said "they are from Tristin." They were displeased and reminded me I was to respect their wishes.

As the months went by, I fondly thought of Tristin and so much wanted to visit him. And now, he is standing right here before me. As we spoke, I felt a rekindling kind of spark. I had a similar feeling for him before. I could sense, however, his difficulty in addressing me. Unlike him during the class, he spoke to me very hesitatingly. Was he disappointed with me? It was as if he stood there for several minutes just looking at me. I watched his eyes as, it seemed, he was studying my face. I did not feel uncomfortable, however. I was happy to see him and thought it was ok for him to reflect for a few moments. Finally, he handed me a three-ringed binder and asked if I would read the content. I asked "what is it?"

He responded "may I not say at this time Olivia?" That was fine. It seemed it was something he wanted me to read outside his presence. I watched him as he left the market. As he did, he removed the green hat and placed it into the trash receptacle. I walked over to where he placed it. A conspicuous patch with the name Tristin was sewn onto the hat. I carefully removed the patch and placed it in the left upper pocket of my blouse. I placed the hat back into the receptacle.

I could not wait to get home to begin reading this mystery material. I promised Tristin I would not open it until I had time to read it. I promised I wouldn't even take a little peek. Once at home, I showered, settled into my bed and hastily opened it to the first page. It was a manuscript for a book. I was completely stunned by the title "Finding Olivia The Book/The Letter." I thought, "what is this all about?" I read the introductory material which included an "Acknowledgment," "Dedication," "Prologue" and "Overview." They took me completely by surprise, but I felt immediate excitement. They seemed to prepare me for the following material, but after reading Chapters I, II and III, my mind rushed back in time and place where we first met. I could not wait to read more. I began to feel saddened, but deeply moved by his words. I was saddened by the matters which were necessary for him to address as a judge and prosecutor. I was amazed at the complexities of his life that drove him. From that night at school, I remember almost precisely, the words he used to describe his motivation and purpose. In a great deal of detail, he expressed "three meanings" and how they were significant to his life and how they should be for others. "Evil flourishes when good men do nothing," "The mass men lead lives of quiet desperation" and most importantly to me, "Love is the active concern for the life and the growth for that which we love." I remember telling him he laid a lot on me at that time. The dramas of his life began to play as I read. I was overcome and actually felt the strong love Tristin had for me. I decided I would write a letter. A letter to Tristin. A letter from my heart. Periodically, it became difficult to write because, from time-to-time, tears filled my eyes and blurred my vision. I could feel the deepness he had for me. I thought "I could have been there for him." The letter began "My Dearest Tristin I remember you being quite confident in your feelings for me. "Love at first sight?" I did not understand why you would say that or how you could feel that way at that time. You seemed too sophisticated merely to give me a line. Somehow, it did not seem to be just a line, but it was unclear to me how it could be true under the true meaning of love.

After reading Chapter IV, I was moved to tears. I watched the video and listened to the music you mentioned. I remember the events as you recounted them. I was extremely hurt as I realized your desperate search for me. When you explained how it possibly could be "love at first sight," I surrendered my heart to you. I read Chapters V, VI and VII and realized your deep appreciation and understanding of events which seem to occur within and without of our realm. In some ways, it seemed you were reading aspects of my life. The extreme cruelty of matters which are necessary for you to address almost daily, were almost unbearable as I read Chapters VIII, IX X and XI. I was again brought to tears as I read "The Green Hat," "Depression & Disguised Opportunities," "Suicide, Sex & Soul Mates," and "Three Wives." I just did not want you to have suffered as you did. I was especially hurt when I realized your willingness to publicly humiliate yourself in your quest to find me. When I read "Why 'Find Olivia' The Three Meanings," I was astonished at the thought you had given to arrive at the interpretation of my name. "Loose Ends & Old Lovers" revealed genuine and honest reflection. Do you love me that much Tristin? It seems, no chapters touched me like it along with "Dreams Come True" and "Found, Forgiven, Forgotten & Remembered." But again, I hardly could bear to witness your suffering because of your love for me. I began to sob, but they were tears of joy. Not only have I now surrendered my heart, I want to deliver it to you. At that time, I sat there and folded the letter. I placed it between the pages of the manuscript. I came to the realization Tristin is my first and only true love. The void I felt throughout the years was because of his absence from my life. It now was clear why I felt the strange attraction toward him the first night I saw him. I thought, "I must see him now." "I must find him now." He did not leave a telephone number. I did not know where he resided. I could not possibly sleep tonight. My parents resigned themselves to the fact there was no stopping me now. I drove away from home in the darkness. I am a firm believer that if you are searching for a lost loved one, you always should return to the place where you last met. I went back to the market which now was closed. For some reason, I went to "Border's." I ran to the second level and searched aisle by aisle. I returned to the first floor and did the same. Frantically, I paced as some of the customers curiously watched. Finally, I returned to the campus where we first met. I ran, in a panic, to every spot where we had spent time. I attempted to enter the main door of the building where we studied together. It was locked. I made my way around the entire building, trying each door. Finally, I found an unlocked door. I entered and ran up three flights to where our class had been held. Tristin was not there. I ran back down to the main floor and out of the building. I nearly was out of breath from running when I heard a voice call out "Olivia, my sweet Olivia." To my relief, It was my darling Tristin. He had been seated on a monumental rock located in an area where he once saw me and walked me to my car. We ran to the arms of one another. We could not control ourselves. I insisted I would not spend any more time away from him. He felt the same, but would not allow us to spend the night together at that time. We reentered my car and just held each other. As we listened to love songs, we must have fallen asleep because the next I remember was awakening in my bed with the manuscript next to me. Frantically, I turned the pages looking for my letter to Tristin. I could not find it. I then realized, I had not written one and I had not gone out the previous evening after all.

* * * * *

CHAPTER XXII

MY REASON
FOR LIVING

* * * * *

Had it not been for the presence of the manuscript, I would have believed the entire story to have been a beautiful dream. I arose almost immediately. I could not seem to get focused, however. The only thing which was certain was I must see Tristin. Should I visit the beautician? What about my nails? What shall I wear? And finally, I slowed down to reflect. Tristin deeply loves me and I deeply love him. I decided to wear a light pastel top with corduroy pants. I then put on my boots. As I left, I grabbed my pink knit hat. I knew I would be able to find him at the courthouse. I timed it where, upon my arrival, it would be near the lunch hour. I did not want him to become distracted, by my presence. Upon arrival, however, no longer could I exercise restraint. I moved quickly into the building and onto an elevator. Once on his floor, I ran to find his name on the courtroom door. I rushed in. There was the love of my physical and eternal life, about to step down from the bench for the afternoon recess. Everyone looked in my direction because of my rapid entry. A deputy sprang to his feet and took a protective posture as I rushed through the gates which led into the area reserved for attorneys. Tristin turned in my direction and almost ran toward me. We embraced as all of those present applauded. I realized this was the happiest day of my life and I do not believe it was happenstance. Tristin and I were destined to be together again. Whether one were to characterize it as "spiritual mate," "soul mate," "karma" or "destiny," we must recognize, from time to time, that power unknown to us is at work.

At this time, I ask you to recall the instances when my parents resisted Tristin's involvement in my life. I loved them and always respected their wishes. A tension was created. In my view, this tension was present for a specific purpose. Let me explain. My parents discovered the manuscript I left lying on a table. They noticed the name "Tristin Dawei." Upon returning home, they asked me to give a physical description of the writer. "Did he have a 2"-3" scar to his right hand and lower back?" I was puzzled. My puzzlement turned to amazement as they related what occurred many years ago. They said during the Viet Nam war, when our family resided in "Saigon," dad was a soldier in the South Vietnamese army. Part of his duties involved guarding the perimeter of the American Embassy there. During the early to mid nineteen seventies, he met a young American soldier who wore a name tag, "Dawei." Dawei was a Lance Corporal in the United States Marine Corps. Dad indicated that although Dawei was a number of years his junior, after becoming acquainted, the two of them worked well together and met for a beer from time-to-time. They became friends. Dad related that as the war began to wind down, because of America's decision to withdraw from the country, the locals were very nervous. It was rumored innocent civilians already were being killed by the thousands in the northern part of South Viet Nam where American troops no longer occupied. Fear permeated the country. It was believed the communists would have no mercy. It was unknown what would happen to those who remained. The fear was everyone who resided in Saigon likely would be characterized as an American sympathizer. Being very concerned for our family's safety, dad made arrangements to get us out of the country. I had not yet reached my first birthday. Corporal Dawei attempted to get dad, mom and myself onto special air transport. He was unable to do so. They resorted to plan 'B' which involved leaving through

Phnom Penn and into Thailand. The trip was dangerous and wrought with many uncertainties. Arrangements were made where we would get safe passage if able to reach Bangkok. My parents and Corporal Dawei knew it would be a long and treacherous journey. Once reaching the Mekong River, the trek became impossible. The wildlife, natives and other perils were just too great to overcome. We were robbed of all our food and possessions at one point. It became necessary to return to Saigon. There was no alternative. It was believed that to continue on, especially trying to cross the river, would not have been possible without food or supplies. Upon returning to Saigon a few weeks after our departure, the city was in such chaos we barely were missed. It seemed no longer was there a rule of law. There was widespread looting and panic. Dad said, with Corporal Dawei's help, we were able to get inside the American compound. Inside almost was as chaotic as outside. Wall-to-wall panicking people. Corporal Dawei was able to get us into the secured areas and near the area which had been transporting American personnel and families out of the country for several weeks. Dad still had his military identification and uniforms. We tried for days attempting to leave in an orderly fashion according to dad and mom. The demand to leave was just too great. We were able to push through the throngs of people with Corporal Dawei leading the way. Once inside, we made it to the roof where a heliport was located. My parents said they could hear artillery in the distance. The panic was real. Finally, the transport vehicles often would not touch down out of fear of becoming grounded by the mob of panicking people. As one of the last flights was about to depart, Corporal Dawei used his American serviceman's status to get the door of the copter to open. It was tightly jammed. My parents said it seemed impossible for anyone else to board. People began to storm the embassy walls. Corporal Dawei pleaded with another American serviceman to allow us to board. The soldier proclaimed there was just no more room. Dawei, seeing no other alternative, hoisted mom onto the craft. The craft was very heavily laden as it became aloft. Dad missed his footing as he tried to enter while carrying me. Corporal Dawei jumped onto one of the landing blades and pulled dad up and was able to get him onto the craft while still holding me. As Corporal Dawei struggled to board, a few rounds from small arms fire pierced his hand and back. Others were able to pull him inside as we departed. Dad, along with others, was able to control the bleeding and stabilize him by the time we reached friendly territory.

It was a tearful, but joyous reunion of Tristin and my parents. The tension no longer was present. No longer was there an impediment between me and the love of my natural and eternal life. I now clearly understand how I was drawn to Tristin. When I first saw him after becoming an adult, he seemed to be someone I wanted to get to know. The powers were at work.

Several months after the reunion, on 5/15, Tristin and I married. I did not believe life could be happier until we were blessed with our beautiful baby daughter 15 months later. She is so so beautiful. She has large American eyes with an Asian influence. Her face is so delicate. She looks like an angel. We named her Kristin. Life could not have been happier for us. I felt the warmth and love of Tristin during the day and night. He was romantic, funny, sometimes silly with us girls and adored us to no end. My love for him was such I never could have imagined feeling for a human being the love I felt for him.

One day Tristin came to me and said he wanted to step down from the bench and spend more time with us. I know him. I can feel him. I am able to sense his feelings. I asked him to share the problem with me. I said "there is no problem great enough for the two of us not to be able to overcome." I began gently to persuade him to share all with me. Finally, after a great deal of reluctance, he imparted news of his health that pulled the carpet from under me. I sobbed. I was angry. "How could life inflict punishment of this degree of cruelty upon me?" I was in a complete state of disbelief and denial. "Tristin," I screamed, "I cannot go on without you." "You are my life." "It is not possible for me to go on without you." "I just can't. *You are my reason for living.*" In his wisdom, as he held me and kissed me on the forehead, he said "Olivia, you must go on for Kristin and you will not go on without me."

I was sickened for days which turned to weeks. It was only with Tristin's help that, finally, I was able to begin functioning again. He helped me to develop strength to go on to raise our beautiful daughter. I promised I would remain strong for her. As the months passed, I saw signs of Tristin's strong body beginning to weaken. I deeply grieved inside. Tristin could sense it and comforted me as often as possible. We were always at each others side.

One day Tristin retrieved the manuscript he had written so long ago. He said "Olivia, It would be an honor if you would complete my work. I said "Tristin, I do not have your eloquence...." and before I could say more, he gently placed his finger on my lips and said "Olivia, you need only speak from the heart."

Finally, it was necessary to hospitalize my husband, my lover, the love of my natural and eternal life. I remained by his side the entire time at the hospital. I refused to sleep in a separate bed. I needed to feel him beside me. Early one morning, 5/16, Tristin's breathing became more laborious. As we held each other, he whispered "Olivia," don't worry, I will love you forever." Those were the last words I heard from my dear sweet spiritual mate, Tristin, as death silenced his lips.

* * * * *

CHAPTER XXIII

THE FINAL TEST

* * * * *

I experienced nearly the same sensation as when I found myself in the hospital and the surgical team desperately was working on my body several years ago before finding Olivia. At that time, I passed out shortly thereafter. This time I did not. As I stood there and watched Olivia and Kristin sobbing hysterically, I realized I was not going back. I saw an attendant cover my head and roll my body out of the room. I felt fine, but I was deeply troubled to see my wife and daughter as upset as they were. My first reaction was to hug and comfort them. As I tried to, I realized no longer did I have a physical existence. I said "Olivia, Kristin, dad is here." I realized at that time, no longer could they see, feel or hear me. I could see, I could speak, I thought, and I could hear. I could not touch, however. I was deceased. At least from life as I had known it. Why am I still here though, I thought. Somehow, I must comfort the loves of my life. What can I do? Where am I going from here? I always thought there would be bright lights and I would, at least, have a shot at heaven. I wanted some answers. No sooner than I said that, I was drawn to a strange place. It is very difficult to describe. To equate it to earthly terms, let's just say an area without boundaries filled with clouds. I was greeted in a clear voice. Actually, it was kind of humorous. You know, like in those Hollywood productions. I was amazed that some of the things humans believe concerning what happens after life on earth is accurate to an extent. Not exact, but somewhat. The voice was from an unknown source. I could not see anyone or anything other than a cloudy environment. I wasn't floating. I did not have wings. I guess I didn't go to hell either.

The voice said, "you were expected here Tristin." "Do not attempt to see more than you are seeing." "You are here the get a few answers to your questions and concerns." "Also, you are here to make certain decisions."

My first inquiry was, "may I ask questions?"

The voice replied "yes, you may." "You may not get an answer to all of them at this time, however." I asked "why am I here?"

Reply "you do not have to be here."

"What are my options?", I replied.

"You have earned the right to enter paradise."

"Right now?", I said.

"Yes."

"What are my other options?"

"The answer to that question is why you are here. There is a final test which you are not required to take."

"Why should I take it then?"

"Be patient Tristin, time is not an issue for you anymore." "Here are the reasons." "During a previous life, you were a lawyer. A very good lawyer. Bailey, Beli, Cochran, Darrow, Gary and the rest could not compare. You were extremely bright, very personable and charismatic. You won acquittals in criminal cases when it seemed impossible. Some of the most notorious and fiendish killers were released because of you. They went out and killed again. That was not your concern, however." "You handled your share of civil matters as well. The class actions made you one of the wealthiest and well-respected lawyers in the country. The corporations hated, feared, but respected you, and the real victims received close to nothing as part of settlements." "You lived the good life." "Nevertheless, you self destructed." "Suicide."

"Under what circumstances would I commit suicide then?"

"You absolutely were correct in your belief Olivia was your 'spiritual' or 'soul mate'. "The two of you have been together a long long time in earthly terms." " Eons, as a matter of fact." "You loved her then as much as you loved her this time around, at least under your definition of love at that time."

"What was wrong then?" "Did she love me?"

"Of course she did, more than anything else in the...." "She truly loved you."

"Why then would I commit suicide?"

"You lived the good life." "The fame and fortune went to your head and took over your commonsense and good judgment, however." "You began to drink excessively and then experimented with mind-altering drugs." "Eventually, you became an alcoholic and developed other chemical addictions." "You always took great care of Olivia, however." "But as much as you loved her, under your understanding of love, after a heavy night of drinking, you caused her to "wear the green hat.'" "You were her first." "She loved you to no end." "You were her whole life." "After learning of your infidelity, Olivia took a tailspin." "She just could not accept the fact as it was." "You tried to fix it." "It was impossible." "You wanted her heart back." "The heart you once had unqualifiedly." "You wanted her back so desperately, you promised you would check yourself into a hospital for rehabilitation."

"Wasn't that good enough?"

"Tristin, please listen." "You checked into the rehabilitation center." "You really wanted to cure the dependency." "You were away for months, however." "During your absence, Olivia committed suicide."

"No, please don't tell me that."

"You want to be reminded of the truth do you not?"

"Of course."

"After her suicide, you took a tailspin. You lost your legal skills due to drugs and alcohol. Your clientele faded. Your wealth and health diminished. All of your properties were lost because you failed to service them. You sank deeper and deeper into alcoholism and drugs. One night in your most miserable state, your committed suicide."

"I was returned to earth?"

"Yes."

"Olivia was returned to earth?"

"Yes."

"Why was I so much older than Olivia this time?"

"You already know the answer to that question."

"I was right?"

"Indeed, you were right." "Even though she predeceased you, you returned much earlier than she did." "She was held in abeyance."

"Many of the Buddhist teachings were correct." "After your suicide you returned under more difficult circumstances as you well know." "Remember all of the instances, even during childhood, when you suffered both physical and mental hardship?" "The freezing days in the snow when you were required to walk or hitch-hike a ride." "Sometimes even late at night." "Standing on the cold streets for long periods." "Almost frost bitten by the time you arrived home." "Recall that it was necessary to work full-time during high school." "When you got off work at eleven p.m., you were too tired to study." "Somehow you managed to graduate though." "That was a must because you were destined to matriculate on to college, law school, become a lawyer and judge." "Remember that mental anguish and suffering." "Even before age ten, do you recall the long cold winters of shoveling snow and the long hot humid summers where you mowed the lawns in order to have lunch money." "Thereafter, the years toiling in the factory and attending college at night." "Remember always being short of funds." "To cap it all off, a few other ingredients were added." "It was decided that a little pigment would be added to your skin in an environment where the 'ugly head' would be of concern." "A little insecurity was thrown in and, of course, the plague of depression to boot." "Nevertheless, nothing could prevent you from judging." "By now, you must know why you felt a desire to fight evil." "It was not coincidence that you became a prosecutor and eventually a judge." "All the killers you got off in your previous life who killed again." "It was not coincidental that incompleteness followed you for most of your life." "Olivia was absent."

"Nevertheless, you lived life, suffered the hardship, discovered and accomplished your purpose, and experienced a natural death." "You are entitled to go on to paradise at this time."

"What about Olivia?" I asked.

"Kind of figured it would get to that." "As you know she must live her life out and arrive here naturally." "Her circumstances, which mostly are mental, look pretty bleak, however."

"How such?", I asked.

"Would you like to take a look?"

"Yes, please yes," I said.

At that time I was returned to the moment of my memorial service. There I was lying in a casket wearing one of my favorite suits and a red tie. The sight wasn't troubling, however. I was kind of glad to have shed that ugly shell, as I used to say. What was very troubling was watching Olivia and Kristin. I needed to comfort them. The voice then said "this is the test you need not take." "Go on to paradise or remain here with Olivia and Kristin."

"What is the test?", I asked.

The voice said "as you know, Olivia must leave there on natural terms." "If she suicides again, which could very well happen, she would be forever lost." "You may try to help her find her way."

"When do I begin," I replied.

"Now, if you would like."

"What do I do. I have no body. I cannot be heard, seen or felt."

"You may have one, if you would like."

"Another body," I thought.

The voice then said, "of course you are free to operate without one." "Although she will not be able to see you, there have been cases like this where the deceased could be heard very faintly and/or felt on occasion." "You realize that already, don't you."

Out of what seemed to be frustration, I replied "what does that mean?"

The voice "you will have to find that out on your own."

"What happens if I take the body?"

"You would physically return and you would have choices." "You may return as a baby, teen, young adult or older." "Sometimes souls are held in abeyance for specific purposes."

I replied "Really."

The voice "really, Tristin." "You know the routine." "You will not recognize her, at least not very well."

"This seems so familiar." "Are you suggesting Olivia returned as a baby in order to help me?"

"You always have been quite astute Tristin." "She returned in a previous life, specifically to help you. The time when you were the great lawyer and made her wear the green hat." "She was sent there for you to find."

"If I return as an adult?"

"You would become the thoughts of an existing person who has yet to discover his purpose." "Again, you would not recognize Olivia very well." "And you must be significantly advantaged." "Eventually, she would realize who you are, in a sense." "Either way, *let's just say, you would be "finding Olivia" or perhaps Olivia would be "finding" you.*

* * * * *

CHAPTER XXIV

I ACCEPTED

* * * * *

I elected to return in spirit only. After making the election, immediately, I found myself in Olivia's presence. She was in bed, but it seemed she could not sleep. She tossed and turned for at least an hour. She got up and began drinking wine. She looked tired and very sad. It seemed, the more wine she consumed, she became more and more saddened. She poured another glass and I became very concerned. She drank very little of any alcoholic beverage when we were together. I then could not believe what I was seeing. She walked over to the safe and retrieved one of my guns. "This is not going to happen is it?" I thought. I watched as she examined the gun. She began to raise it. Frantically, I screamed, "Olivia, put that thing away." "Get rid of it." She did not acknowledge my presence. She then placed the gun onto the table. She began drinking more and more. She laid a bottle of sedatives before her. I thought, "oh no, you're not going to do that." I tried with all my might to push her hand away from the bottle. I tried to take the wine away. I could not. I felt completely helpless. She went down to the wine cellar for more wine. I screamed in desperation. "Olivia, baby, you have had too much, please don't." She lost her footing and fell. I screamed, "oh my sweet baby, please." I tried with all I had to assist her to no avail. Out of desperation, I tried to enter her body and become her thoughts. I could not. I pleaded with her to return upstairs without getting more wine. She lay on the floor for several minutes. She then stood, turned around and returned upstairs. Her mouth and nose were bleeding pretty badly. She sat down and stopped the bleeding with a wet cloth. As she sat there, I was right there beside her. "Lady" was playing. It seemed to remind her of our being together. She screamed out "you are not here beside me." I screamed "yes, I am, baby, I am right here." She cried harder and longer than I had ever seen of her. I was grief stricken. I must help her. She began sipping more wine. I pleaded with her "Olivia, please no more, please." I began to think perhaps I was having some type of impact on her because she put down the wine glass. She sat there crying and saying "life is just too hard, I cannot go on." At that time I was in a purely panic state as she reached for the gun again. She lifted it and looked at it for several minutes. All the while, I was trying to push the gun away. It was useless. I could not. I was screaming at her out of pure terror. "Please, my sweet baby." "Olivia, I am here with you." *"I love you with all my heart and soul and I always will."* "Please put it down." She lowered it and then began looking at the sedative bottle again. I tried holding her. Again, I pleaded with her. I screamed. I did all in my limited power to persuade her to put it down and return to bed. To my relief, she put it down, stumbled to bed and fell asleep. I watched over her throughout the night.

The next morning, she managed to shower and prepare for work. I tried to say she needed a good breakfast. Instead she took three aspirin. I walked with her to her car. As soon as she started the car, the system began playing "Lady." It played over and over as she drove to work. She cried almost the entire time. I was so hurt while powerlessly watching her every move. After struggling through the work day, she drove toward Border's bookstore in the pouring rain. It was gray. The day looked dreary and depressing even if one were in a happy state. I was concerned as she sobbed most of the way to the store. I pleaded, "God, please help her." "Please intervene here." At that moment there was a sunburst and out of nowhere, a beautiful rainbow appeared. Her crying subsided. She parked. We walked toward the store. She stood there looking at the rainbow. Although her eyes were red and slightly swollen, she was so so beautiful. I wanted to comfort her so badly. I stood behind her and put my arms around her and said "Olivia, you are not alone."

As time passed, and the more I was in her presence, at least spiritually, the more melancholy she would become. Every day, I wanted to touch her. I would lie beside her in bed. I would be with her all the time. I discovered then, that when I did say or do something, it seemed she felt or heard it somehow and for and instant, she would feel better. In the long term, however, my presence seemed to keep her living in the past. I did not want her to continue to grieve my passing. I was doing fine. Even if I were not, I would not want her to grieve. She had suffered too much. Upon realizing she needed more than my spiritual presence to get through this lifetime, I prayed that I be permitted to take on a body. Immediately, I was returned to the cloudy area. I said, "if I must go through witnessing her lifetime with events anything akin to what I witnessed, I would have a heart attack if I still had a heart." The voice said "if you take on a body, it would be irrevocable and you would be required to live out that life irrespective of what may happen to Olivia." Without hesitation, I asked to return as an adult.

* * * * *

CHAPTER XXV

THE RE-TRANSFORMATION

* * * * *

Hello! My name is Kyle D. Kristianson. At the risk of appearing immodest, I will take a moment to describe my physical appearance and certain character aspects. I am blonde with blue eyes. I stand at approximately six feet. My face, well let me say that many people say I am very handsome. I'm not so convinced of that nor do I care. I am forty-five years of age. I received an M.D. and specialized in psychiatry. I completed a JD program for informational purposes only. I never practiced law. I have worked for several years as a clinician. I got lucky on certain business investments and became financially well off. I think I have a good heart and a tremendous capacity to love. For some reason which isn't quite clear to me, however, I never married. I guess I never met the right person. You see, I have this feeling deep inside that *the instant that I 'recognize' her, that very second, the pieces of my life finally will fit.*

Seeking more completeness in life, in addition to practicing psychiatry, I became a minister. My objective is to live life with God being a part of it. I want to help others to do the same without the exclusivity doctrines. What that means is, I do not emphasize one's particular faith or religious title, such as Buddhism, Christianity, Judaism or other faith, over another. We assemble to worship, discuss our similarities and differences in belief and let God take it from there. In spite of certain procedural differences, we believe there is the greatest power of all powers that controls all, has defined light from darkness, regulates time and eternity, has unlimited love for mankind and the deepest disdain for evil. We call it God. I use the term 'it' out of respect, because the power is not a 'he' or 'she' or any other human designation in my view. Sometimes we must use a human pronoun, however, in order to equate to people.

I have been blessed with a church and large congregation that is growing in leaps and bounds. I came to realization that life had been so extremely good to me that I needed to give something in return. I discovered the ministry to be a natural. Monday through Friday, I am busy counseling patients on mental illness, alcoholism, chemical addiction, depression, esteem and other issues and aspects of human behavior. Generally, I found the work to be rewarding. However, there are those heartbreak cases that require help from above. This realization was another motivating factor to move into the ministry.

On Sundays, I provide an after-service meal for anyone who would like to worship and dine with us. The only requirement being, that you sit through an hour or so of teachings. This is one of my favorite days of the week.

I was seated at my desk in the medical office the other day when my receptionist informed me that my next appointment was present. I asked that she be shown in. Her name was Olivia Dawei. I read her chart and determined her to have been a victim of attempted suicide. I am always very concerned about these patients because it is very difficult to determine what would cause one to go to that extreme and because of the finality if they were to succeed. I greeted her upon her entry. She responded, but did not make eye contact with me. As a matter of fact, she looked toward the floor most of the time. At that time I realized I had my work cut out for me. I ordered a complete physical and rescheduled her. I wanted to eliminate any physiological cause for her disturbance.

Approximately three weeks later, she again entered my office while keeping her head and eyes directed toward the floor. I had her medical reports. Without thinking, I believed I was imparting good news when I said something to the effect that she would live to a ripe old age. Immediately, it occurred to me that I committed a faux pas with words I could not retract. At that moment, she looked up at me very quizzically. This was the first time I really was able to see her face. She was forty something, and with the exception of being a little on the underweight side, she was strikingly beautiful. You ever see someone and it seems you somehow were familiar with the person? That was the sensation upon first seeing her. I had other strange feelings as well. As time went on, I felt almost desperate in my need to address her problems. I wanted to get her back on the road to good mental health.

* * * * *

CHAPTER XXVI

LIFE AFTER TRISTIN

* * * * *

It was three years after the death of my love and spiritual mate Tristin before I was able to complete the writing of "Finding Olivia." Tristin's words were so clear, it was as if he had spoken them yesterday. He said *"Olivia you need only speak from the heart."* With those words, I knew it was possible to complete it, and I promised him I would. What was not contemplated was the extent of the devastation of my life upon his passing. The first two years, were surreal. The pain, the disbelief seemed to have kept me in a fog. Almost every night thereafter, I found myself awakening and screaming out "please let this not be true" only to find that, indeed, it was true. Had it not been for my responsibilities to Kristin, I would not have gotten out of bed. It seemed I could not get one thought on paper without completely falling apart. I shelved it numerous times. The task seemed to have become insurmountable. I needed to overcome it, however. I promised him I would. During the third year, as I began to write, it was if I had begun living life all over with him through the writing. It became such that in my secret thoughts, I dreaded completion of it. I wanted to stay with it. I remember the day when the publisher said it would be on the shelves of the major bookstore chains. It seemed I was returned to square one after sitting in a Border's and reading it again.

Continuing life without Tristin would have been a total nightmare had it not been for our darling daughter Kristin. She almost was grown up then. Throughout the years, I could see his expressions on her face and hear his voice through her's from-time-to-time. Those moments brought happiness and sadness. Sometimes I struggled to stay composed during Kristin's recitals and other school activities. On countless occasions when parents accompanied their children, I saw the distant stare in Kristin's eyes as I realized how badly she wanted her dad to be there with us. It always brought tears to my eyes. It was as if watching her suffering through the years magnified my grief and suffering. It seemed never would I overcome the loss of Tristin.

Kristin seemed to bury herself in her studies. It was as if she did not want a free moment. She kept busy at something to escape, it seems. Throughout junior and senior high school, her only interests seemed to be her academic studies and music. She became so dedicated to both, she excelled in school and became recognized throughout the state for her violin acumen. Early on, advanced placement courses were recommended and in time, almost every course was college preparatory. She graduated with a grade point average well above 4. During her valedictorian address, I cried when she saluted her father and me.

Tristin encouraged Kristin to pursue a profession other than law. His feeling being if she were to become a lawyer, although she would be able to assist others with solutions to their legal problems, necessarily and routinely, she would be exposed to the problem. That over time, the exposure could lead to unhappiness. He encouraged her to develop an interest in the dramatic arts, an area that he had a strong interest, but decided to practice law. It was an example of, as he would say, *when one selects a certain course, another necessarily is foregone.*

After Kristin's high school graduation, she enrolled in a prestigious school for dramatic arts in New York. She earned it, she wanted it, but somehow, I hardly could bear to see her leave. I felt truly alone at that time. My dad had gotten up in age. Dad hardly could remember anymore. I left my work and tried a hand at writing. As life goes, mom then passed. I discovered there was nothing left of my heart from which to write. After several months, I was in such a depressed state, I developed a habit of never leaving the house. Not even to visit my dad. I ordered groceries and food through a delivery service. I then began to keep all curtains and windows closed. I did not want to see anyone anymore.

My longtime friends were seeming to become an annoyance, always inquiring about my well-being. On one such day after receiving a call from my best friend, I consented to her visit. I had not seen her for so long, it seemed we needed to become reacquainted. She seemed very concerned and I knew she meant well. She said it appeared I had lost a great deal of weight. She said the luster seemed to have left my eyes. I could sense she was hurt over my personal appearance. I expressed to her, I just did not feel like continuing on with life. She would not accept that. She insisted that we go out for lunch or dinner. Although I had not left the house in months, finally, I acquiesced at her insistence. After lunch, she insisted that we meet at least once per week for lunch or dinner. She would not permit my refusal.

I recall an occasion when she asked and then insisted that I attend a social gathering with her. Neither mentally nor physically did I feel I was up to it. At her insistence, however, I reluctantly agreed to accompany her. Upon arrival, I felt very awkward. I recall being aloof and inattentive during conversation. After dinner, an adjacent room was opened to continue the evening with dancing. No way was I interested. I asked my friend if we might return home. Somehow she came up with what seemed to be legitimate reasons for delaying our departure. I realized it was not her intention to cause me discomfort, but it was her way of causing my reintroduction to society. After being asked to dance on two occasions and refusing, I became very uncomfortable. But as uncomfortable as I had become, seeing my friend having such an enjoyable time, I could not bring myself to raise the issue again. As I watched the couples on the dance floor, I decided I would have that glass of wine offered by my friend. As I sat there, somewhat more relaxed, Celine Dion's "Power of Love" began to play. My mind immediately rushed back to my first dance with Tristin. What he called our first real dance together. I remember him taking my hand and leading me to the dance floor. As he held me, through his eyes, I could see the unequivocal love in his heart. At that point, no matter how hard I tried to compose and restrain myself, I began crying aloud. Within seconds, my friend was there and we left for home. My friend became so concerned for me that she asked if she could spend the night. I assured her all would be okay. Before leaving, she insisted on calling later and that I answer my telephone. I assured her that I would.

Because of the unexpected throw back in time, I found, I could not sleep. I left the bedroom and headed for the family room. I decided to pour myself a glass of wine. Then another and another. I located Tristin's CD collection that I treasured. I played "Lady" over and over again. After about two hours and two bottles of wine, I was thoroughly under the influence of it. I had sedatives. I do not recall how many I took, but I knew it was several. I entered the bathroom and filled the tub with warm water. I brought another bottle of wine with me. I undressed, sat in the tub and listened to "Lady" as I sipped the wine. I screamed out "life is just not fair." "I am too weak to bear this extreme and unrelenting pain." I screamed "Tristin, my darling Tristin." "I recall your teachings of suicide and returning under worse circumstances, but I cannot live this life any longer without you." At that time I used a steak knife to cut deeply into my wrist, rested my head against the back of the tub, submerged my arms and passed out.

The next I recall was being in a hospital with physicians frantically working on my body. I watched them. I was not in it, however. I felt at peace, but strangely alone. The only thing I remember thereafter, was being in a recovery room several days later. As it turned out, my friend felt so strongly about leaving me alone that night, she telephoned. Getting no response, she drove back to my home and could not get me to respond to the door. She was able to get the patio sliding doors at the rear of the house to open. She notified emergency services.

* * * * *

CHAPTER XXVII

POWERS AT WORK

* * * * *

State law required that anyone who was a patient because of a suicide attempt was required to undergo a minimum number of psychiatric counseling sessions or be involuntarily committed for 72 hours for psychiatric care and observation. After remaining in the hospital for two weeks, I recovered from the physical injury and was cleared for release. I signed the commitment to attend the counseling sessions. I was assigned to see a doctor of psychiatry named Kyle Kristianson.

After entering the anteroom of his office, I registered with the receptionist. It was not long thereafter, the receptionist indicated the doctor would see me. Actually, I felt apprehension and embarrassment as I was being led into the office. The doctor stood and greeted me as I entered. I noticed a nameplate on his desk that read "Kyle D. Kristianson, M.D." I wondered what the "D" stood for. I continued looking down as I responded with a faint hello. He began speaking almost immediately. For some reason, his words seem to make me feel a little more at ease. He said "you do not have to speak to me at all if you do not feel like doing so." "You need not look at me as well." "Of course, you may speak with me and look at me as long as you want, if you care to." " I'm not saying I am anything you would want to look at for a long time and we can talk about anything you would like to talk about." "Well, you know what I am trying..." He trailed off in mid-sentence. His comments struck me as a little humorous. I did not know if it was intentional, however. But from his tone and demeanor, immediately, I felt good vibes toward him.

After a brief introduction, he ordered a complete blood work-up, physical examination, e.e.g. with brain scan, and rescheduled me for a time after the results would be available.

He wanted to eliminate any physiological or chemical basis for my behavior. "That visit was not that terrible," I thought as I left the office. I never looked directly at him.

Three weeks later, I returned for the second session which I realized would be more substantive. I sat in a comfortable chair as he remained behind his desk. I continued looking down as he went over the medical reports. He said "all is normal." "You should live to a ripe old age." His remark seemed just a little humorous under the circumstances. Thinking perhaps I did not hear him correctly, I looked up at him for the first time to see if he was being serious. When I did, I saw a most kind, gentle and understanding face. As a matter of fact, it was the type of face that was very pleasing and easy to look at. It seemed he wanted to take back those words, but then he said "You wouldn't want to come back and do this again would you?"

I said "pardon me?"

He then repeated "you wouldn't want to come back and do this again would you?" I was bewildered because he seemed serious and, of course, the comment was consistent with what I believed may be a real possibility. For some reason I said "have we met before."

He said "yes, don't you remember?" And before I could think he said "three weeks ago." "Remember." "You were sitting there and I was sitting here." For the first time in some time I felt like laughing.

At our next session, we began discussion of depression. He said it is common and widespread. That the ordinary course of treatment would be counseling and/or chemically. He advised that too often patients opt for a chemical course hoping to get from under the tremendous and heavy burden of it immediately. "Sometimes this works, sometimes it doesn't," he said. He then began to inquire how long I suffered depression. "Was it triggered by a specific tragic event or a series of events?" He inquired. He asked me to reflect back to much earlier in life before meeting Tristin. Was I happy? Somehow he was able to prompt me to reveal a lot more than I believed would be possible or that I had been willing to impart. Soon thereafter, unbelievingly, I disclosed some of the most secret aspects of my life to a person who, just a few weeks earlier, had been a total stranger, I thought.

After several weeks of counseling therapy, I was persuaded that counseling without drugs was the appropriate course for me. I did not desire chemical therapy, if avoidable. Somehow, I was beginning to feel better. Not out of the woods in my mind, but better. At some of the sessions, it seemed this man was strangely familiar. The more he said, the more I wanted to hear. There came a time when I looked forward to the sessions. It seemed he enjoyed counseling me. During one session he said "sometimes men do not have the answers." I was hoping he wasn't going to leave it at that. He then said "*the incompleteness* you spoke of earlier, you know, the void?" "Sometimes it only can be filled by a power much greater than man." I was completely stunned. I said "we never discussed an incompleteness or void."

He responded "are you certain of that?"

I said "I am quite certain." "The term is too significant for me to have forgotten any discussion of it."

He then apologized by saying "forgive me, it must have been a different patient." I sat there not believing what I just heard. I could sense he did not believe it to have been another patient.

He floored me again when he said *"I bet you dollars to donuts"*... He then trailed off and stopped abruptly. I said "please complete what you were saying."

He said "what?" "I did complete my thought." He then said "I think that will conclude today's session, unless you have other questions or concerns." As I left the office, I could see him watching me through the reception window. I thought, "a mysterious, but good man."

During our next session, his probing questions almost forced me to come to terms with my sadness and despair. He took me as far back in time as I could remember. I recalled unhappy times. I said "people use to say I did not smile enough." He said "perhaps there was not a great deal to smile about." He guided me step-by-step from early life to the time I first met Tristin. He asked what was it about Tristin that caused my attraction. I explained, that initially, there was just something that drew me to him and I did not know why. But finally, there had been a previous meeting between us. At that time I related the experience of Tristin and my parents in Viet Nam. We went from our first meeting through marriage and birth of Kristin. We then began discussing Tristin's death. I explained every moment leading up to his last words to me. By that time, I was crying my eyes out and he made me feel there was no reason to hold back. My mind then began to rush back in time. Out of the blue he said "do you believe the two of you are spiritual mates?" I could not answer, I was so shocked by the question. He then said "if you are, there is no need to go back to the past." You will see him soon, provided you are not successful at self destruction." I looked at him in awe. I thought, *"this man is not from this earth."* I went home with feelings of joy because his comments seemed to validate what I had hoped and believed all those years. I cried at times, but it seemed only because I was becoming impatient for time to move on.

During our next session, he said. I believe we were able to accomplish a great deal. I believe you no longer are in need of the intense sessions. With that, I almost panicked. I had begun to rely upon and trust this person more than any other since Tristin's death. I thought, "how could you leave me like this." I felt as if I was being abandoned as I turned to leave the office. He then said, *"if you are spiritual mates, don't worry he will love you forever, the powers are at work."* I felt chills run through my body as I hurriedly left the office. I needed to reflect upon the totality of what had occurred since meeting Dr. Kristianson.

* * * * *

CHAPTER XXVIII

"FINDING TRISTIN?"

* * * * *

I had more than fifteen months of sessions with Dr. Kristianson. Initially, I felt alone and abandoned after his indication they no longer were necessary. But after an adjustment period, I was beginning to feel more normal. There was not one day, however, that I did not think of my darling Tristin. I began visiting with friends again. I even had the courage to fly over to the east coast to visit Kristin. As always, we had a wonderful time together. Kristin then informed me of her good fortune. She would be living in Paris for the next several years to continue with her music and creative arts career. I was deeply saddened. My thoughts were that I never saw her enough when she resided in New York. I knew, however, I must let my baby go and I wished her well.

After returning home, I seemed to feel a little more normal. I thought it was time get involved again. What does a woman of my age do? School or community service? Volunteer, perhaps? What about my spiritual life? I always had been unsure in this area until meeting Tristin. Even though we did not participate in a great deal of indoctrination, we recognized the importance of a spiritual life. When speaking with my best friend on the subject, she suggested we attend the nondenominational congregation that recently had been given a great deal of local press because of its involvement in community service. I thought, it may be a good place to begin.

On the next Sunday morning, my friend picked me up and we proceeded to the church. We arrived a little early and plenty of seating was available near the front. We sat there paging through some of the materials that were located in the racks on the backs of the bench seats. I then became utterly stunned and felt chills run through my entire body as the minister took to the podium. It was Dr. Kristianson. My best friend was floored when I imparted the news to her. A few months had gone by since last seeing him. He never mentioned being a minister. I sat there and began thinking, he knows almost my entire life. His countenance was aglow as he addressed us. Because of the size of the sanctuary, which by then was at capacity, I did not think he realized my presence. He then said *"you are here today because God answered my prayers."* It seemed he was looking at me as he was speaking. His sermon touched me like no other. He knew my life inside and out. I was of the impression that somehow I was special to him. He touched my heart at that time, somehow.

After service, we adjourned to the dining hall. He went from table to table and greeted all in attendance. I was excited, happy, nervous and experienced many other emotions as he arrived at our table. He looked at me and said "I prayed for the day that you would be in attendance." I realized at that time that I occupied a good deal of his thoughts during the last several months. What was unknown was whether his comments should be viewed in a doctor/patient context. After greeting the other tables, he thanked everyone and welcomed us to the next Sunday's service. As my friend and I were leaving, Dr. Kristianson walked up and asked if he might speak with me. My friend and I looked at one another. He offered to drive me home. On that cue, my friend turned and almost dashed to her car, leaving me with him. He asked if we may go out for coffee. I inquired whether it would be a professional or social visit. He said "our professional relationship as doctor/patient has ended and I would like to see you socially before a priest/penitent relationship might get underway." I readily accepted. He found a quiet café where we could converse somewhat in private. In a switch, I said "doctor, you know so much about my life and I know very little about yours." Before I could say more, he said "there is not a great deal to tell." He explained he had been involved in a serious automobile accident, was hospitalized and in a coma for several months. That his recovery was not expected. But then, somewhat of a miracle occurred. One without medical explanation. That he recovered completely with the exception of slight memory loss. He explained it was after his recovery that he had a strong desire to seek the ministry. He said it was as if his entire perspective on life had changed. He said it was as if he had been born anew. He then said "Olivia, would you please call me Kyle?" "May I call you Olivia?" I agreed to both. It occurred to me that it was a date, of sorts. I had not been out with anyone other than Tristin once Tristin and I met. Kyle and I enjoyed spending the time together getting to know one another. He drove me home and asked might we go out again real soon. I agreed.

Once at home, however, I began to feel a little guilty. I looked at the photos of my darling Tristin. Immediately, I felt sorry and decided I could not visit again with Dr. Kristianson. I did not hear from him however, until the next Sunday at church. I wondered why he had not telephoned me at least for me to relate my change of heart. During his sermon, he said *"look to God for answers when you have life altering questions."* For some reason, immediately, I had another change of heart. After service, he asked whether I would like to go out for dessert. I readily accepted. During this visit Kyle said he was happy our counseling sessions had ended. He said "I prayed daily that one day you might show up at our church." He explained he was reluctant to invite me because the relationship could easily have shifted from one professional relationship to another. I said "you are suggesting a relationship between us?"

He said, "I am suggesting...well...er...well...yes a relationship of some sort."

I replied "are you able to define the type of relationship you had in mind?"

He said "Olivia, I know how, seemingly, unkind the years have been to you." "I firmly believe things happen for a reason." "I fear, however, that since I had been your doctor and"..."you know, you hear of instances where a patient is in a vulnerable state and"... "it has happened in cases like where the patient mistook feelings of gratitude for something else."

I said "what are you trying to tell me?" "I really would like to know."

At that time, He said *"I refuse to live in quiet desperation."*

I just could not believe my ears. I sat there stunned at that comment, but I did not want to interrupt what it appeared he was about to say.

I said "please complete what you want to say."

He said "Olivia, I loved you the moment I laid my eyes on you." "I know it sounds like the cliche, 'love at first sight', an idea that I do not believe in, but the feeling has overwhelmed me since meeting you."

Not believing any thing I was hearing, but, for some reason, now wanting to believe, I just sat there shaking. Deep in my heart and soul, it was what I wanted to hear. My mind then immediately went back to Tristin. But before I could begin to feel guilt or compose myself, he said "perhaps it was just love all along."

Chills ran through my entire body. I could not believe what I was hearing. I looked at him and he exuded complete honesty.

I could not help but say "do I know you?"

Jokingly, he said "perhaps we met in a previous life." I asked him to take me home. We drove there in almost complete silence. After entering my house, I thought, "shall I ever see him again?"

The days seemed to become an eternity. I listened to "Lady." I became angry at Tristin for leaving me. I looked at his photos and read his letters. I was confused and torn. I prayed.

Finally, on Saturday night, to my relief, to an extent, Kyle telephoned. He asked if I would see him. I indicated I would. No sooner than I entered his car, he said *"Olivia, is it possible that you could love a man like me?"* I knew at that time that I could and that the powers were at work

* * * * *

CHAPTER XXIX

TOO MUCH TO TAKE

* * * * *

Kyle and I became almost inseparable. We enjoyed theater, musicals, movies, breakfast, lunch, dinner, and all other activities together. It seemed we never wanted to be apart. What had not happened, however, was physical intimacy. Kyle was pretty cognizant of matters generally. Months had gone by. He never once pushed me. He was fine tuned and sensitive to my feelings for Tristin. He was patient. One night after walking me to my door, however, he said "are you ready for me to kiss you?"

Instantly knowing at that time, that I knew him, I said "Kyle, it is possible that I could love a man like you." "I am ready for you to kiss me." He stood there in complete silence. It was as if he began wondering. He looked at me and asked "do I know you?"

I said "I believe you are beginning to recognize me."

He asked "what?"

I left it at that. He kissed me.

I never believed it possible that I could love a man other than Tristin. Yes, he was always in my heart and I believed he would forever be there. Somehow, however, I loved Kyle. We married. We had a great life together. We remained inseparable.

One evening Kyle and I were reminiscing about the early days of our meeting. He was reminded of the circumstances of how we met. He looked at me with all seriousness and, it seemed, out of fear. He said "Olivia, promise me that under no circumstances would you ever again attempt suicide."

I responded "Kyle, I am beyond that." "How could that be possible now." "I love you."

He said "no, I would like for you to promise me, make a commitment to me right now."

I searched my heart and soul for the briefest moment and said "that is my commitment to you Kyle." "No matter what circumstances may confront me, never again would I attempt suicide."

Throughout the next few years, it was absolutely astonishing the many occasions, Kyle used the same expressions as Tristin. Life was good again. One evening, however, Kyle was late coming home. It was unlike him not to keep me apprised of his whereabouts. I had not heard from him for several hours. At about nine o'clock p.m., I telephoned his medical office. I then telephoned his office at church. I tried his cell phone. I began to become very concerned. This just was not like him. I drove to his office. Then to the church. Starting to become a little frightened, I began calling out his name. I ran to the church office and opened the door. It appeared as if Kyle was resting his head on his desk while seated there. As I walked toward him, I said "honey, is everything okay." He did not respond. I gently shook him. He fell to the floor. I panicked and began beating on his chest after noticing his color was pale. He was not breathing. I dialed 911. I screamed "oh, God no." "Please don't let this happen again." I was hysterical by the time paramedics arrived. The team went to work. They could not revive Kyle. I could not believe this was happening. They placed a blanket over his face. I felt as if I was experiencing a nervous breakdown. Another medical team forcibly strapped me to a gurney. I had become hysterical. They intravenously administered sedatives. I felt myself lose consciousness.

After regaining consciousness, I cried day and night. I had no appetite. I could not sleep. I hoped and prayed this was just a horrible nightmare. It was not. It was real. I could not make it through Kyle's memorial service. I fainted and later found myself under a doctor's care again. I was heavily medicated. Eventually, I became catatonic. I sat and stared for hours on end without food or sleep. I could not live anymore. My mind was tormented to the highest degree a human could tolerate without losing sanity. Finally, after intense chemotherapy, I regained lucidity. I persuaded medical practitioners that I would be able to return home and function. Once at home, however, the ghosts haunted my mind. The pain was so great, it was too much for any human being to handle. I struggled through each day and night, periodically screaming in pain. The intensity was unbearable. I had absolutely nothing to live for. I could not hold down food. I over sedated, but not to the toxic level. I consumed wine day and night. I regurgitated on a regular basis. The house had become a mess. No longer could I prepare meals. It seemed, I never was hungry. I existed on sedatives and wine for the most part. I promised Kyle. No, I made a commitment to Kyle, never would I attempt suicide. Nevertheless, on numerous occasions I considered the consequences. Surely, it could not be worse than the pain I was experiencing. Finally, my body had become so weak, I began to experience physical pain all over. I played "Lady" constantly, day and night. Alcohol and sedatives were my diet. I cried throughout the night and screamed "oh, God, why must I suffer so?" I passed out.

* * * * *

CONCLUSION

MERCY IS FOR THE MEEK

* * * * *

I found myself in the cloudy area. I wondered why I was there. I asked "why am I here?" The same voice said "you were returned."

I said "why?"

The voice said "your time was up."

I said "again?"

The voice "Correct."

"What about Olivia?" I said.

The voice said "certainly expected to hear that." "Would you like to see her?"

"Please, yes, of course."

"The voice said "take a look."

I could not believe what I was seeing. Olivia hardly appeared recognizable. She was as thin as a rail. Her lips were dry. Her eyes no longer had sheen and were blood red. They were swollen, almost shut. She did not look focused at all. I heard her crying. She said "no matter how bad matters become, I will not commit suicide." She sobbed and sobbed. She said "please God, please don't let me suffer like this anymore." "I will myself to you." Her torment seemed unrelenting. No sleep, no peace. Physical agony now had set in.

I said "please don't let her suffer like this anymore." *"Please don't give her too much to handle."*

"I beg for mercy on her." "It is deserving in this case." "It would not be misplaced." "Please let me return and take her place." "Let me return for her suffering." "I am willing to give my heart and soul for her."

"Are you sure?" said the voice.

I responded *"is love not the active concern for the life and the growth of that which we love?"*

The voice responded *"do you love her that much Tristin?"*

I responded " with all my heart and soul."

Within moments, Olivia was standing right beside me. In the distance, I saw her body lying peacefully on the bed. We turned to one another, smiled and said *"I love you with all my spiritual heart and soul."* As the clouds cleared, we realized we only had awakened from a dream and never had left paradise after all. *We thought.*

* * * * *

* * * * *

A LETTER
TO OLIVIA

* * * * *

"Finding Olivia," also is intended as letters. One my heart yearns to receive from her and one to her from my heart.

* * * * *

Olivia, I seek your recognition of me. As you know, firmly rooted in the recognition, I must have your heart. I do not insist on having it for my security, but because it would be the only way to insure complete happiness for you. I need your complete unequivocal exuberance in the giving of it.

Do you recall the evening I explained the three meanings? My purpose was to help you understand my fabric and uncover your feelings for me. Why one would spend a lifetime at a career that contemplates hardship. To combat evil? I feel certain you appreciate the compulsion felt by me from deep inside. My purpose on earth is to 'find you'. *The height of my love for you is the extent of my disdain for evil.*

The second meaning "leading life in quiet desperation." My choices were quite clear that night. Should I have let you go without sharing the meanings with you? I am happy you permitted me the opportunity. Do you recall when I discussed Fromm's teachings? I was speaking from my heart and hoping you were listening with yours. You must realize there was not one word uttered to you that evening I believed to be untrue. I am able to repeat it a hundred times with consistency because of the accurate portrayal of my feelings for you. I truly am sorry that I overwhelmed you.

If your decision is "Tristin, go away, it will not happen in this lifetime," while I would be saddened, I would savor those moments I did spend with you for the remainder of my life. Before I go, however, I would ask you Olivia, what do you believe your purpose here on earth to be? Are you pursuing it?

Public embarrassment for me? Saving face? "Too risque" as they say? Olivia, to completely know my heart, you readily would realize those considerations pale in comparison to your importance to me. There is nothing more important than you being part of my life here on earth and forever. For that reason, I made this commitment based on faith. One that is embodied in another Fromm observation. He said *"to love means to commit oneself without guarantee, to give oneself completely in the **hope** that it (our love)will produce love in the loved person." "Love is an act of **faith**, and whoever is of little faith is also of little love."*[35]

As I pondered how I could articulate my love for you Olivia, it occurred to me neither written nor verbal expression nor songs are adequate, nor sufficiently eloquent, elegant or precise, no matter how well crafted, to convey my true feelings for you. Words only are single-dimensional. They cannot express the depth and other dimensions of my love for you. It lies beyond our five senses.

I would like to refer back to the inquiry "how do you know Olivia to be your eternal mate?" I recognize you as such because the depth of my love has produced an enlightening and exciting energy within me which makes it unmistakable. The time from meeting you again and all the days thereafter, has been the most important period of my entire life here on earth. There absolutely

[35]

The Art of Loving. Page 118.

is no uncertainty, hesitation or incompleteness with you. Never have I experienced anything like the fullness you have added to my life.

Olivia, there is one more thing I would like to share with you before I close. For the most part, I completed writing "Finding Olivia The Book/The Letters" many weeks ago. At the risk of interrupting the flow of the text of "The Letter," I decided to add the italic highlighted portion written this day. It is now late November. *Earlier in the book, you were melancholy one morning. The day was gray and rainy. While driving to work, you listened to "Lady." During "the meanings" portion, there was a sudden sunburst and beautiful rainbow that seemed to warm your heart. Why it occurred to me to make that part of your experience while composing it at that time, is unknown to me. I ask you to reflect back and recall that during the past several months, in the area where we reside, there virtually had been no rain or cloudy days. However, today, as I drove to work, and necessarily I must drive by your city, it was strangely cloudy. It began to drizzle. I was listening to "Lady." Near the playing of "the meanings" portion, a rainbow appeared that was followed by a sunburst. I am unsure what this means. However, I must say this particular morning, I felt a little melancholy as I pondered whether I ever would see you again during this lifetime. The sunburst and rainbow brightened my day.*

If I never 'find you' or see you again while on this earth, you always will hold the most special place in my heart. A place no other possibly could occupy. *Thank you for being the sweetest dream I ever have had.*

Yes, Olivia, I have two former wives, but *"you are my first love."*

Tristin

* * * * *

* * * * *

A LETTER TO THE READERS OF "FINDING OLIVIA"

* * * * *

The purpose for this letter is to thank all who chose to read "Finding Olivia." Its purpose also is to seek your input on a number of the areas which were discussed. I formatted a form for your responses or you may devise one of your choosing if you care to participate. To begin with, I would like your input, especially from women readers, on what areas, generally speaking, I may have overlooked in attempting 'to find' Olivia. If I am fortunate enough to find her, I would like to be finely tuned to her needs. Would you ladies and gentlemen kindly help me out in this area with your comments? You may reach me by writing to me at: Dawei Productions. P.O. Box 1550 Hollywood, CA 90078-1550.

Secondly, I would like to receive feedback on the following topics: Abortion, Death Penalty, ACLU, "Evil Flourishes," "Quiet desperation" and "Love is the Active Concern" principles. I would like an indication of AGREE or DISAGREE. You may provide any comments on thoughts you may have on those subjects following your response. In addition, I would like to hear your comments on the viability of the following proposal. Although I am uncertain at this time how the effort may be structured, my intent is to use the feedback to make your views known to The White House and Congress. Please provide the name and office address for your Senator and/or Congressperson. I would expect to receive responses over a period of time, therefore, I will report poll results to Washington every ninety days or thereabout. Please be patient in that regard. I am employed full-time. If you would like to make a donation to cover expenses such as extrapolation from collected data, formal reporting of results, publication of some sort, postage, office expenses, etc., please send either

$0.05, $0.15, $0.55, $0.56, $1.55, $1.56, $5.55, $5.56, $15.55, or $15.56. I pledge to use any donations received for the stated purpose. Finally, I would like to ask whether you believe a book should be written by Tristin that would discuss the feedback? If so, would you agree to utilization of your comments? Would you be willing to reveal your identity for publication? You may include a snapshot of yourself. As you know, publication of all comments would not be possible or feasible. I personally will read all comments and select which may be included in any publication.

My kindest and warmest regards.

Tristin K. Dawei

In the spirit of "The Three Meanings," and in order to determine prevailing views, please answer the following questions:

(1) Evil is flourishing in our country.

( )Agree. ( ) Disagree.

Comments:

(2) George W. was on the right course in seeking to abate evil.

( )Agree. ( ) Disagree.

Comments:

(3) The ACLU, in fact, is eroding our liberties.

( ) Agree. ( ) Disagree.

Comments

(4) The ACLU is out of touch with my feeling and beliefs.

( ) Agree. ( ) Disagree.

Comments.

(5) Therapeutic abortion never should be permitted.

( ) Agree. ( ) Disagree.

Comments.

(6) Therapeutic abortion should be permitted in very limited cases such as rape, incest or health of the mother.

( ) Agree. ( ) Disagree.

Comments.

(7)   Realizing a line must be drawn somewhere, and therefore almost arbitrarily, it is reasonable   to allow therapeutic abortion until the end of the first trimester.

( ) Agree. ( ) Disagree.

Comments.

(8) Therapeutic abortion should be permitted through the ninth trimester, as is the law in many states.

( ) Agree. ( ) Disagree.

Comments.

(9) The death penalty is appropriate in some cases.

( ) Agree. ( ) Disagree.

Comments.

(10) The death penalty never is appropriate.

( ) Agree. ( ) Disagree.

Comments:

(11) Most women and men "lead lives of quite desperation" on issues such as those discussed herein.

( ) Agree. ( ) Disagree.

Comments.

(12) You enjoyed reading "Finding Olivia?"

( ) Agree. ( ) Disagree.

Comments.

(13) A book should be written concerning the majority view based upon poll findings on the issues.

( ) Agree. ( ) Disagree.

Comments.

(14) Tristin or someone should contact Washington to express the prevailing views.

( ) Agree. ( ) Disagree.

Comments.

(15) "Love is the active concern for the life and the growth for that which we love."

( ) Agree. ( ) Disagree.

Comments.

* * * * *

GLOSSARY OF TERMS

-A-

Abortion, Therapeutic,
The surgical, mechanical or chemical removal of a fetus from the womb, ordinarily performed by a medical doctor in a hospital setting.

Afghanistan, .
Arab populated country located in the middle east, bordered by Iran, Pakistan and Russia. During the late 1990's and early 2000, it was occupied by a fundamentalist religious group called the Taliban. Suspected of hosting terrorist training activities and groups, i.e., Al Queda. Believed to have provided support for groups whose purpose was to sponsor international terrorism. Believed to have been involved in the destruction of the World Trade Center, NY, USA, September, 11, 2001. The Taliban was ousted from Kabul, the capital city, by military force of the United States Government during 2001-2002.

American Civil Liberties Union, (ACLU)
Organized by Roger Baldwin and others in 1920 to champion civil liberties.

Armstrong, Neil,
July 20, 1969 successfully piloted space shuttle Apollo II to the moon, becoming the first human being to step onto the moon's surface.

Autopsy Surgeon,
A forensic scientist and medical doctor trained to determine the cause of death in human beings and testify in court concerning those findings.

-B-

Beijing,
Formerly called Peking, the capital of the People's Republic of China.

Benson, Herbert, MD,
Professor of Medicine, Harvard Medical School. Conducted research on benefits that may be derived from regular intervals of meditation.

Beyond a Reasonable Doubt,.
Standard of proof required for conviction in criminal cases in the United States.

Brooks, Garth,
Popular country singer/songwriter, 1990-2000's.

Buddha, Buddhism, Buddhist,
Buddha was a religious teacher and philosopher who lived in India, c563-483 BC. He founded Buddhism which is a religious philosophy with primary belief that right thinking and self abnegation will lead to Nirvana, a divine state. Buddhist practices Buddhism.

Bush, George W.,
43rd President of the United States. Lost popular vote to former Vice-President Al Gore by 500,000 votes during 2000 general election. However, won majority of electoral college votes, winning the Presidency. The election nearly gave rise to a Constitutional crisis. The State of Florida, where the brother to the President was Governor, provided the 25 electoral votes needed by both sides for majority of electoral votes. Authorized military action in Afghanistan and Iraq shortly after the attack on the United States.

-C-

Camarena, Enrique,
Drug Enforcement Agent of the United States who was captured and tortured to death while carrying out covert activities in Guadalajara Mexico, 1985.

Christianity,
Religion stemming from the teachings of Jesus. Its sacred scripture is the Bible. Jesus is the son of God. Jesus died for our sins by crucifixion. Grace is central to the religion.

Cochran, Johnnie,
California Attorney-At-Law, successfully defended Oranthal James (O.J.) Simpson against charges of murder of Nicole Brown Simpson and Ronald Goldman. Handled other high profile cases including clients such as pop singer Michael Jackson and actor Todd Bridges.

Coup de Foudre,
A sudden intense feeling of love. Love stricken like a bolt of lightning.

Coup de Grace,
The final blow that delivers death to the victim.

Croce, Jim,
Genres: Rock music.
Style: Soft rock, singer/songwriter.
Died in airplane accident September 20, 1973.

Cutler, Howard, M.D.,
A diplomate of the American Board of Psychiatry and Neurology.

-D-

Deon, Celine,
Popular ballad/pop singer during 1990's to present.
Immigrated to United States from Canada.

Denver, John, (John Deutsendorf)
(1945-1997).
Popular country/pop singer, especially during 1970's, until
death caused by airplane mishap during 1997, off the coast
of California.

Due Process of Law (Substantive & Procedural),
Due process refers to a party or entities right to remedies
required by federal and state constitutions.   Often,
procedural rights involve the right to a hearing.   During
such hearing a party ordinarily would have a right to
present evidence, including witnesses, tangible items,
etc., (or a defense), confront and cross-examine witnesses
and a right not to incriminate oneself. Substantive rights
refer to protection of and enforcement of laws such as the
requirement that laws regulate a legitimate governmental
interest. Double jeopardy could be one such right.

Durst, Robert.
Texas millionaire acquitted of murder in a well publicized
case in Galveston in 2003. Suspected of a killing in Los
Angeles and of killing of his first wife in New York.

-E-

Eagleson, David,
Served as an Associate Justice of the California Supreme Court from 1988-1991.

Eastwood, Clint,
Actor, former mayor of Carmel, California.

-F-

Federal Rules of Criminal Procedure(FRCP).
A body of statutory procedural law that applies to the practice of law before the federal courts.

Forensic (Pathologist, Scientist, etc)
Methodology, collection, research, investigation, the product of which is for use in court.

Fromm, Erich, (1900-1975)
Psychologist and Author. "The Art of Loving," "The Art of Living" are among his well-known publications.

-G-

G, Kenny, (Patrick G. Kenny)
Instrumentalist and recording artist known for his distinctive sound.

Garcetti, Gilbert I. ,
Former District Attorney of Los Angeles County. O.J. Simpson case prosecuted during his tenure.

Gibran, Kahlil,
1883-1931, Poet, author, philosopher and artist. Born in Lebanon, his poetry was translated into more than 20 languages.

Gore, Albert,
Former U.S. Senator from the State of Tennessee. Vice-President during the Presidency of William Jefferson Clinton. Although winning the popular vote by 500,000, he was defeated by George W. Bush in a controversial decision by the U.S. Supreme Court.

Goldman, Ronald.
Friend of Nicole Brown Simpson. O.J. Simpson was charged with his murder and acquitted by a Los Angeles jury.

-H-

Hussein, Saddam,
Former dictator of Iraq. Ousted by United States military insurgence during 2001-2002. Believed to have been responsible for training, aiding and advancing terrorism throughout the world.

Hitler, Adolph,
(1889-1945). Chancellor, dictator and leader of Nazi Party of Germany. Promoted the Aryan race as superior to all ethnic groups. Responsible for mass murder of millions of Jews and other ethnic minorities throughout Europe. Committed suicide with wife in 1945.

-J-

Jackson, Alan.
Country Singer/Songwriter. Popular during 1990's-present.

John, Elton.
Love Song, CD. Tract 2, "The One."
MCA Records, 1986. Popular British rock/pop singer who debuted in the U.S. during 1970.

Johnson, Earvin, "Magic"
National Basketball Association Star-Guard. Led the Los Angeles Lakers to five championships in the 1980's. One of the sports 1st international players. Devoted a great deal of time to youth and AIDS related activities.

Johnson, Lyndon Baines.
(1908-1973). Became the 39th President of the United States upon the assassination of President John F. Kennedy on November 22, 1963.
(1963-1969). Popularity greatly diminished during Viet Nam conflict. Declined to seek reelection in 1968.

<u>Jury of Peers</u>.

A constitutional and statutorily mandated right by federal and all state governments. Peers refers to a fair cross-section of one's community. In general terms, a venire or panel available to try the case should reflect the demographics of one's community.

-K-

<u>King</u>, <u>Rodney</u>,

Gained international notoriety after a private citizen video taped several members of the Los Angeles Police Department beating King. The footage seemed to portray King being under control and not resisting law enforcement commands at the time of the beating.

-L-

<u>Lama</u>, <u>Dalai</u>.

Tibetan leader of Buddhism. Enthroned in 1949, but fled after revolt against Chinese government which began occupancy of Tibet in 1950. Exiled to India.

<u>Lee</u>, <u>Bruce</u>. <u>(Lee, Yuen Kam)(1940-1973)</u>

Martial art's expert and U.S. film actor. Although born in San Francisco, he spent most of his childhood in Hong Kong. Died in 1973 of a brain edema.

Liu, Chi-Jen.
Internationally known as the Grand Master of Feng Shui
and Yin-Yang. Prominent artist, author and philosopher.
Speaks English, Chinese and Vietnamese.

-M-

Madden, John.
Former Head Coach of Oakland Raiders. Led team to
victory over the Minnesota Vikings during Super Bowl
XI. Winning record made him the best head coach in
the league. Later became sportscaster and nominated for
'Emmy' award 15 times. Recently, joined Al Michaels on
"Monday Night Football."

Mandarin.
Mandarin Chinese is the official language of the People's
Republic of China.

Mekong River/Delta.
2600 mile river that originates in Tibet flows southward
through China and Laos, along the border of Thailand,
through Viet Nam The Mekong Delta is a wide fertile area
of the river in South Viet Nam before it reaches the China
Sea.

Mesmerize.
A patient treatment technique developed and practiced by
Dr. A.F. Mesmer. It involved inducing a hypnotic State.

<u>Modus Operandi</u>.
Refers to method of operation. The term usually is associated with crime, criminal activity or behavior.

-N-

<u>NASA (National Aeronautics Space Administration)</u>.
Founded in 1958 by President Eisenhower, its primary mission is nonmilitary space exploration and research.

<u>Ninjakun</u>.
Berkeley California artist who developed the book cover for "Finding Olivia, The Book/The Letters."

<u>Nixon, Richard M. (1913-1994)</u>.
37th President of the United States. Ordered the withdrawal of American forces from Viet Nam. Widespread student protests occurred during the secret bombing of North Vietnamese military sanctuaries in Laos and Cambodia.

-O-

<u>Opportunities Turned Around/Disguised Opportunities</u>.

-P-

<u>Perception</u>.

Perception through sight, smell, taste, hearing and touch. Extra Sensory, Spiritually Guided. Perception beyond taste, touch, smell, hearing and sight.

Phnom Penn.
Capital of Cambodia. A branch of the Mekong delta links it to the China Sea.

PHO.
A popular style of Vietnamese cooking especially for preparing soups and stews.

Pinyin.
A phonetic system created to aid in learning Mandarin, Cantonese and other Chinese languages and dialects. The system converts Chinese language characters to English phonetics.

Pol Pot.
Ruthless leader of communist Khmer Rouge, he captured Phnom Penn and caused all inhabitants to evacuate the city. He was responsible for the deaths of about 2 million during his reign of terror. He was driven out by the Vietnamese.

Prestidigitation/Prestidigitators/Prestidigitationists.
Un-huh, you're back here. You must be smart. Let me give you a test. It is called 'Free Word Association'. Do not cheat. After I ask this question, blurt out the first word which comes to your mind. Ready? What is the moon

made of? For those of you who passed, do you see how absurd the result was? A prestidigitator is an expert at prestidigitation. Prestidigitation is defined in Webster's dictionary as the slight of hand.

Note: the test may not have been fair for those who were not raised in America. Many American children were taught the moon was made of cheese.

-Q-

-R-

<u>Roe v. Wade</u>,

-S-

<u>Saigon</u>.
Capital of South Viet Nam before falling under communist control during 1975. Renamed Ho Chi Min City after communist takeover.

<u>Santa Monica, California</u>.
Coastal city suburb of Los Angeles situated near, Bel-Air, Beverley Hills, Brentwood, Westwood and other affluent sections of Los Angeles County.

<u>Shakespeare</u>, William. (1564-1616) British poet and playwright. English literature is recognized internationally for tragic plays such as "Hamlet," "Othello," "McBeth,"

"Romeo & Juliet," "Anthony & Cleopatra" and many comedies such as "Much Ado About Nothing," "As You Like It" and "The Merry Wives of Windsor."

Shanghai.
Located near the Yellow Sea, it is China's largest City. It is important for industry education and commerce.

Simpson, Nicole Brown.
Former wife of O.J. Simpson who was the victim a brutal knife attack that caused her death. O. J. Simpson, former husband, was acquitted of her murder by a Los Angeles jury in 1995.

Simpson, O. J.
Professional football player for the "Buffalo Bills" and "San Francisco 49ers" teams. Charged with killing Nicole Brown Simpson and her friend Ronald Goldman. Acquitted of criminal charges. Found liable by a jury in a civil proceeding.

Strait, George.
Popular country singer/actor during 1980-present.

Taliban.
Political and religious military group which eventually took over most of Afghanistan, including its capital city Kabul. Responsible for brutal repression of its citizenry, especially women. Provided haven for Osama Bin Laden,

alleged leader of Islamic militants accused of worldwide acts of terrorism.

Taupin, Bernie.
Songwriter for many of the hits performed by Elton John during 1970-1990.

Teng, Teresa. (Teng, Li Jen).
Chinese singer of ballads who performed in Mandarin, Cantonese, Japanese, English and other languages. Died of asthma attack after performance in Singapore during 1997.

Thailand.
Formerly Siam, its capital is Bangkok. Pop. Est. More than 61 million. Bordered on the east by the Mekong river.

"Thinker" Sculpture.
Sculpted in 1880 by French sculptor Auguste Rodin.

Third Eye.
Concept developed by Liu, Chi-jen.

Thoreau, Henry David. (1817-1862)
U.S. Poet, writer, naturalist. His masterwork was "Walden" which was 1st published in 1854. Another famous work published during his lifetime was "A Week on The Concord and Merrimack Rivers."

"Three Meanings."
Characterization by author Tristin Dawei given to famous observations/postulates by Burke, Thoreau and Fromm.

Tyson, Michael.
Former criminal street gang member whose talent was discovered while an inmate at a reform school. Youngest heavyweight champion in the sport of boxing, at age 20. Held title from 1986-1990. Convicted of rape in 1992. 1997, his licensed was revoked for biting off an ear of defending champion Evander Holyfield.

-U-

Universal Pictures.
Purchased by Music Corporation of America (MCA) during 1960. Major motion picture, television and record company of the U.S.

-V-

Venue/vicinage.
The place or county where events took place which give rise to a legal action.

-W-

World Trade Center.
Commercial complex had been located in Manhattan, N.Y.
They were the world's tallest buildings until surpassed by
the Sears Towers in 1972. September 11, 2001, they were
intentionally rammed by hijackers of commercial airliners
resulting in total destruction of the complex.

-X-

-Y-

-Z-

INDEX

Goldman, Ronald 10
Gore, Albert 5

H

Hitler, Adolph 22
Hussein, Saddam 5

J

Jackson, Alan 26
John, Elton 36, 108
Johnson, Earvin "Magic" 9

K

King, Rodney 10

L

Lama, Dalai 16
Lee, Bruce x
Liu, Chi-Jen x, 55

M

Madden, John 36
Mandarin xiii, 30, 50, 55, 85,
    92, 124, 131, 136, 138
Mekong River 159

N

NASA 65
Ninjakun 143
Nixon, Richard Milhous 6

P

Perception 55, 67
Phnom Penn 159
PHO 49, 123

Pinyin 131
Pol, Pot 22
Prestidigitation, Prestidigitators
    13

R

Roe v. Wade 17

S

Saigon 7, 158
Santa Monica, California 9
Shanghai 92
Strait, George 116, 122

T

"Thinker" Sculpture 143
"Three Meanings" 153, 212
Taliban 5, 19
Taupin, Bernie 36
Teng, Teresa 47
Thailand 159
Third Eye 55, 56
Thoreau, Henry David 34
Tyson, Michael 12

V

Venue/Vicinage 10

W

World Trade Center 5, 28

About The Author

The author received his baccalaureate and juris doctorate degrees during the late 1970's. Thereafter, he served as a lawyer in public prosecution. As a prosecutor, he handled major crimes that often involved the death penalty or decades of imprisonment.

For thirteen years, he served as a judge in courts of limited and general jurisdiction within the United States, handling both criminal and civil cases. Due to government regulation, he cannot be specific regarding the court whereon he presides.

The author studies Mandarin Chinese as a hobby and hopes to become fluent in the language within the next few years. He would like to serve as an advisor to the Chinese justice system.

Printed in the United States
20671LVS00007B/1-45